P9-BYO-804

Sons
of
God

by

christine mercie

DeVorss Publications
Camarillo, California

Sons of God
Copyright © 1954

All rights reserved. No part of this book may be reproduced, stored, or transmitted in any form without permission in writing from the publisher, except by a reviewer who may quote brief passages for review purposes.

ISBN: 978-087516-059-7
Twenty-Fourth printing, 2008

DeVorss & Company, Publisher
P.O. Box 1389
Camarillo CA 93011-1389
www.devorss.com

Printed in the United States of America

DEDICATION

To all those who have so unselfishly given of themselves, their time and substance, that this book might come forth to bless humanity.

Sons of God

Chapters

I.

I DIP INTO THE EARTHY

So this was the end of the trail? Could it be possible that this filthy dive, called a room, was the place I was meant to occupy when I was brought to Los Angeles? Or was it just a test to see what I would do about it? Since I, seemingly, had no choice in the matter, the only thing that counted was how I reacted to a situation so desperate.

I gritted my teeth to keep a firm hold upon myself as I looked into the dingy depths of reeking degradation. The room actually seemed to be whimpering in the shame of its dregs. It was a personification of the evil, the tears, the heartbreaks and misery that had been shed with past violence into its, perhaps, protesting embrace. This repulsive room seemed as ashamed to have me gaze at its reeking stench, and almost as shocked, as I was.

I would have fled in shuddering horror had I had any choice in the matter. It was only the knowledge that every test was for a purpose, and was really a privilege, if I could only accept it as such, that gave me the power to step over that threshold. It was the only comforting touch in the whole situation—this knowledge that all diffi-culties are sacred assignments because they are the only real stepping stones to progress and the prog-ress lies in the comprehension of their purpose.

I had come so very near to failing once. It was the memory of that failure that made the present situation bearable. Anything was better than failure. Anything! It was this thought that bolstered my spineless courage with backbone. It completely subdued the "yellow streak," giving me the power to whistle in the dark, though with a trembling uncertainty.

This vile little room contained an unclean wash bowl in the corner with a huge, clumsy medicine cabinet above it. There was a wobbly chair, a dingy window that looked out on a dingier brick wall and a bed as repulsive as a swine's wallow. And even as I stood with an involuntary shudder of dismay I saw the cockroaches scurrying from behind the medicine chest, down to the dripping water faucet.

Roaches in the daylight! A mild convulsion went over me as I realized that if there was even one or two bold enough to appear in the day-light, there would be armies of them at night. The floor, the walls, everything would crawl with them.

My natural instinct demanded that I flee. And ordinarily I would have done just that, but my being there was not ordinary. It was the most extraordinary event of my life. I had no choice in the matter. I reminded myself that I should be grateful for even this repulsive, dubious shelter. And by being "grateful" I did not mean that resigned self-pity of a martyr's attitude. It had to be the deep, sincere gratitude coming spontaneously from the depth of my soul.

For a moment the desire for deep gratitude was only a desperate desire without strength or vitality. It was a dead body without a soul. I struggled hard to give it light but the only reaction was an almost overwhelming urge to throw myself and weep with the hysterical abandon of a small child. So great was the struggle it seemed the very walls were swaying in on me.

Then, quite suddenly, there must have been shining legions for I was quite at peace. Don't ask me why, or how. Only this book can explain that or even a shadow of it. But suddenly there was the power to reach down into the inner recesses of my heart and pull forth that singing song of gratitude. And with it came a thousand waving banners of victory. I stood in complete triumph.

This song of gratitude was the most beautiful, the most stupendous thing that had ever touched my life. At first it had been only a game I had practiced with myself when things became too rough. It seemed to make them bearable. It sort of lighted the dark, shadowed places and gave me the power to breathe. That was at first. Then suddenly the game had turned into something very real and very powerful. I became like a small radio that could tune itself in with the great symphony of the universe. It was a song of such utter glory that it could in an instant banish darkness.

It seemed that the only difficulty I was still having with it was the ability to remember that I could turn it on. That room had almost overwhelmed me and made it impossible, for a moment, to remember the power of that singing song of glory, the song of everlasting gratitude, the song of infinite power. I wasn't sure whether I was making that song a very part of me or whether I was becoming that song.

That room portrayed the very bottom of all existence to me.

But after one reached the bottom? What then? I knew with the commencement of that inner song that after one has reached the bottom it is impossible to go lower. After one has struck the very lowest depths one would have to begin to climb. The rising would be as necessary as the descent, unless one just gave up and wallowed.

I knew that the easiest thing in the world to wallow in is self-pity. Even crime and remorse are not as easy to wallow in as feeling sorry for one's self. If one refuses to make any effort to rise it is possible to remain at the bottom until death brings release—or, perhaps, an intensified continuation of the bitterness. But no one can remain at the bottom who will make even the slightest effort to climb. In fact, it is as difficult to remain on the bottom as it is to lie on the bottom of a lake or swimming pool, or river.

I had ceased striving once. That once had been enough. Nothing could ever make me just give up again. Someway I would climb out of the muck of that filthy room, and until I did I would try to enjoy it. Impossible? Nothing is impossible. Other people lived in such rooms—well, maybe they only existed. And right there I decided it was just about the best thing that could have happened to me. And that proved to be true.

I gave my last five dollar bill to the fat, lazy Chinese boy waiting expectantly in the doorway.

I have learned since that most of the low-grade hotels and apartments in Los Angeles are being taken over by the Chinese and Japanese. Many of them, like the mother of the lazy youth before me, could not even speak English. I realized that to some of them these reeking, filthy bug-ridden holes must have seemed like Paradise. While to

me it was the very bottom of the bottom. I had
never before in my life been in a place so completely, utterly impossible.

And yet I *was* grateful for it. The gratitude
became more real after the first shock had worn
off. I was grateful to get a place of any kind,
really. It was a miracle to me that I could get
one for only five dollars a week. It was the winter
season and every available dwelling, apartment,
room and dive in Los Angeles was occupied.

More than that. It was my last five dollars. What
I would do when that one week was up I did not
know. But suddenly that song of gratitude within seemed to make me vaguely detached from it,
almost as though it were no concern of mine. It
was as though the power to rise above the situation
completely had been given. It was almost as
though it was not I who was occupying that hideous
little room, as though I was standing apart watching the drama without being in any way connected with it.

The door closed behind the fat boy who had
left without a tip. I doubt if he had ever been
given a tip by any of the poor occupants who
dwelt in those dreary rooms. The first requisite
to existing in such a place would be the utter in-
ability to give out tips.

After the door had closed I sank down upon the
chair that was in an almost hysterical state of

collapse. I took out my two remaining one dollar bills—all I owned in the world, and wondered what would happen next. Those two bills, no matter how hard they tried, could not possibly take me through the two full weeks it would require for me to find work and receive a pay check. Besides food, there would be another week's rent due in just seven more days. Another five dollars!

Most individuals in my position would have been worried. And according to all rules I should have been. But I wasn't. I knew I would never go down to that desk and ask for credit. I had never asked for favors in my life, not from anyone—and it could not start here. If I accepted any favors when I had no money it would bind me to the place when I did leave. And deep in my soul I knew that obligation would not be required of me.

It was that inner knowing that I would not grovel, nor lose my self-respect, nor need to, that made me aware that the song of glory had become a symphony. I guess it was that song of gratitude that gave me the knowledge that I would never need to grovel. I rejoiced that I was no longer striving desperately to clutch that song to me, like a drowning man a straw. It was holding to me, carrying me along on its wings of light.

I unpacked my suitcase. The few articles of clothing I possessed look luxurious and strangely out of place in that shabby little desperation stop of the earth's "down-and-outers." Only I was neither "down" nor "out." As I shook the wrinkles from my clothing I caught myself humming a merry little tune. I smiled softly to myself. I smiled even as I noted the dusky light of evening increasing the crawling little insects on the walls.

I knew in the gathering dusk that my hunger was not as important as my peace of mind. Part of my precious two dollars was to go for disinfectant. And I was grateful that I could get it. And that gratitude wasn't a forced song out of my mind. It was a singing gratitude right out of the very depths of my heart.

Later I filled the wash bowl with the diluted disinfectant and poured it, with the one chipped drinking glass, behind the heavy, hanging medicine cabinet. It ran down the dingy, streaked walls and an army of bugs rushed out, curled up and died before my eyes.

I soused the solution into the frayed gaps of the rug, around the mopboards, into the corners, and along the moulding. And even as I battled I saw bugs come in under the door, bugs drop through a pipe hole in the corner of the ceiling and my feeling of victory vanished. The whole six-story building of clutter and filth, divided into little bug paradises, called rooms, needed renovating, disinfecting, fumigating, purging—perhaps burning. Out in the hall, a little distance from my door, open garbage cans crawled with vermin. No matter what I did it would bring only temporary relief. But even temporary relief was worth fighting for.

I soaked toilet paper with disinfectant, then placing my suitcase on end upon the chair, teetered myself precariously upon it and stuffed the opening around the pipe. I soaked my one and only towel in the solution and stuffed it along the bottom of the door.

I was barricaded. No more bugs!

At least that was what I thought before I finally dropped wearily into bed. And within a few minutes other bugs began to crawl. I got up, turned on the light and they scurried. I lifted up the under sheet and gasped in horror. In all my life I had never seen anything so utterly, completely filthy as that huge box, inner-spring mattress. I can't describe it. I shall not try. That white sheet was completely desecrated by the very sacrilegious assumption of what it sought to hide. It was like the robes of the priesthood or clergy seeking to cover the putrified evils of a lost soul. Such attempts have been made but the results are even more revolting than crimes that are out in the open.

With a violent physical shuddering I again spread out that desecrated sheet. Leaving the glaring, unshaded, drop light burning I sank down again upon the sodden stench completely exhausted.

I was at the end of my resources and was so infinitely weary.

Thus ended this strangest of all strange days for I must have fallen asleep before my head even touched the pillow.

II.

THE ETERNAL DAY

That strangest of all strange days had really started on the evening before.

I had been sitting on a clean hilltop at the edge of Yuma, Arizona, watching a blazing sunset paint the sky in flaming glory. At my back the Colorado River was murmuring its mysterious complaints to the evening hush. It was complaining at the banks for crowding it in. It was grumbling about its weakened condition because men had so often dammed its course. It murmured about its weariness as it recalled in a hazy sort of way the long, lonely miles it had traveled in its life-time as it journeyed onward toward the sea. It grumbled and murmured to itself like one grown very old, who forgets, mayhap, that he is not alone. Each mile had been a year, and its journey a lifetime. It was much closer to its journey's end than it realized for its heaven of rest was very close—very close indeed.

But I was not turned toward the river, nor listening to its complaints, nor giving ear to its wandering reminiscences of its dancing, frolicking, sparkling childhood.

I was as absorbed in my own thoughts as was the river in his.

I sat watching the sky, aflame with splendor. And my mind was following the fiery footstep of the sunset in its eternal rounds as it circled the earth.

I yearned for a plane that would travel at just the right speed to keep that sunset before me for at least one full, twenty-four hour span. I was viewing with new eyes the breathtaking wonder of the sunset eternal—the sunset that is always and forever and forever — the eternal sunset shaking out its blazing blankets to bed down the earth where day goes tiptoeing out. It was the never-ending sunset that I was really seeing for the first time, not just the minute portion of it before me, holding its place for a fleeting moment. I was viewing in my mind that never ending sunset that goes on and on, winging its way in its eternal rounds as it keeps stride with the sun, circling the earth forever and forever, without stopping, without ending. The breathtaking wonder of there always being a sunset upon some area of the globe struck me for the first time. Above and through the clouds, across the seas, over the mountains, along the desert sands, always and forever the sunset—never ending.

And always and forever the dawn preceding the sun—the dawn rolling back the blankets to awaken the day.

Thus the dawn, the day, the sunset, the night, each following the other in their eternal rounds of never-ending existence, circling the earth in their ever rotating journey. They each exist completely and fully at all times, together, yet individually apart. The dawn and the sunset perhaps are but the soft kisses, or the delicate handclasp between the night and day—their meeting place of lingering caress.

Always somewhere is the day, somewhere the night; and somewhere the day and twilight holding them together in a loving, momentary, breathtaking caress of ecstasy.

It may not be new days, as we have thought, blossoming forth with each dawn, but the same eternal day over and over, returned to give us one more chance to try again—and yet again. If we could but lift ourselves high enough to gain the great perspective who knows but what we might find that time is not; that it has never been. It could be quite possible that yesterday, today, tomorrow and all time is but one—eternity in its eternal rounds.

These thoughts turned my meandering mind backward to my mother and the difficulty of the life she lived. I recalled that in my maturing youth

I had thought how utterly impossible my mother's life seemed to me. I knew that I could not live a life like hers, not in a million years, I couldn't. Her life, to my mind contained everything that was undesirable and impossible. And then, even in my youth, I had somehow been given the understanding that if I had lived my mother's life it would not have been as my mother lived it, but as I would live it, therefore, it would not be her life at all, but mine. And it is possible that we were each living the same life, she in her way, I in mine. I knew as I watched that sunset that my life would have been as impossible for my mother to have lived as hers would have been for me. We each had to express life in our own way, with our own equipment or lack of it, and according to the vision in our souls.

Such had been a portion of my thinking as I had waited for the sunset to turn its back and usher in the early evening stars, for there was a deep purpose in my being there on the desert sands at dusk. It was much more than a thought, or even a desire that had brought me across the continent. It was a feeling which contained the whole purpose and meaning of what had been— and what would be.

III.

"SPEAK TO ME ACROSS THE DESERT SKY, IN EVENING, AND I WILL HEAR"

Yes, Ronnie, I had journeyed across a continent so that I could speak to you across the evening skies. The feeling that if I could but stand alone on the warm desert sands, where first we met, I would feel again the gentle touch of your hand. I had to whisper to you when only the stars kept watch. I had to call your name. I had to tell you of my love.

I had been so sure that I could speak to Ronnie across the great infinitude of space 'twixt here and there, if only I could kneel alone in the deep solitude of a desert night and feel that silent benediction of the evening skies, for surely the dusky twilight is but a benediction, a symbol of eternal peace. I had traveled from New Jersey because I had suddenly become so sure that I could speak his name above the hushed silence of the breathless solitude. My very voice would caress the night with such pleading warmth it would have to carry my message to the uttermost ends of the universe, if need be.

My confidence to reach Ronnie thus came after my grief had spent itself, and after my sniveling self-pity had arisen from the shame of its selfishness, and after my sorrow had clothed itself with courage, and my broken heart had been offered upon the altar of complete quiescence.

And so I whispered softly and my voice breathed out caressingly across the evening sky: "Ronnie, Ronnie, dear, I must talk with you! Please listen! I must share with you the things that have beaten themselves into my soul, these new, hidden things that lie new-born within my heart, things which were conceived in such great sorrow.

"Darling, I've learned to banish the great grief and the darkness of despair. It isn't that I think of you less, or love you less. I think it may be that I love you even more. Or that I am growing more worthy of your love. The hopeless, tragic heartbreak has become a source of inner strength, of love perfected, of being able to let you go— and yet having you closer. I must tell you about it.

"When you went to Korea, Ronnie dear, I had a premonition that you would not return. You had it too, for back of your bantering, half jesting words, 'Christine dear, when you get lonely just speak to me across the desert sky, in evening, and I will hear,' there was a message so earnest, so serious I could not fail to understand.

"Part of me went with you, Ronnie. I knew

when you were killed for part of me died. I knew you had gone before I received the news from your mother. I knew it the instant it happened. I was as sure of it then as I am now. Such is my love for you. Such has it been from the beginning. Such will it always be.

"For months I only wanted to die. I longed— I even prayed for death. Something inside of me was already dead, my heart, my soul, my mind, perhaps a portion of all three, and only this unhappy body went on in an unreal agony of existence. It was that way for months. I could not work. I could not think. I could only go on feeling and even that was in a dead, half-paralyzed sort of way.

"And then, Ronnie dear, an angel's wing must have brushed my cheek, or your kiss breathed upon it, or God reached out a healing finger and touched my soul—I know not what. I only know I was alive again, that life's responsibilities were again mine, and that I had to make good, for your sake.

"It was not an exuberant, glorious aliveness to which I awoke, Ronnie, It was more like a painful awakening to face life's difficulties that had somehow accumulated during the interval of shock and recovery. It was a return of my thinking faculties and then I was ashamed suddenly of my selfish sorrow. I was not ashamed of loving you so much. I would always love you like that. But

I was ashamed of the selfish abandon of my grief. It was unworthy of you. I realized I was a selfish coward, rebellious and ugly in my heart. I was not grieving altogether for you, Ronnie. I was mourning mostly over myself, the bleakness of *my* life without you. Quite suddenly I knew that you were all right! That you would always be all right! No matter where you were you would be all right, standing always triumphant, above the storms and all vicissitudes.

"Ronnie, darling, I'm sorry for my selfishness and a grief so unworthy of you, truly I am. I would have called you back, crippled, blinded, broken in body, just to satisfy my selfish sorrow instead of letting you go on triumphant, free.

"I realized your medals of bravery had been bestowed, not so much because you had given your life, but because you had lived each moment of it, even the very last, torturous one, being big and noble and unselfish. It was those moments of living that counted. Yes, it was those last glorified moments of complete super-living that made the dying so very great.

"I know now, Ronnie, that it is not glorious just to die, though I still look forward with longing to it. But I know that it is only how one dies. No. I don't think even that is correct. It is only how one lives, for it is only the living that could possibly glorify death, or overcome it.

"Two thieves were crucified with Christ, thousands had been crucified before, and many since His time. Yet no others glorified such a death as He glorified it. It was only the way He lived that glorified the shameful way He died. Even as the life you lived, even in those last moments, as you saved your regiment, glorified completely your going. And so I realize that death can only be exalted by magnificent, courageous living.

"We hear, Ronnie, of giving our lives for our country, a work, an ideal, a religion, a loved one, or a way of life—and we think it means dying. How blind we've been, really. Dying takes only a few minutes—at most a few hours. Living takes a lifetime. To really give one's life for any cause would call for the dedication of that living, breathing, daily consecration of conscious existence and awareness—every year—every month—every week —every day and every moment of living.

"It is this supreme dedication, Ronnie, that I must give. It is the only thing that is worthy of your glorious ideals, your courage and your love.

"I give my life, Ronnie! Not by dying! But I give my living life! Every vital moment of it! Now! And forever more!"

Then with the tears gathering in my eyes and coursing down my cheeks I added a little postscript to my message, for suddenly I felt that

Ronnie had heard—and now the very heavens were listening in silent anticipation.

"I promise that I shall never again complain! No matter what happens! I shall glorify every sorrow, sanctify every shred of suffering, glorify the pain, and light the darkness with love. And upon the holy altars of heaven I offer up the burden of my broken heart. If ever again the unbearable burden of it tries to weigh me down, O Lord, I shall lift my heart in praise to you."

Those had been my words sent across the desert sky as the deepening dusk sped upon its way to hold its pace in the flying footsteps of the sun.

What happened next is most difficult to describe. It was as though a mantle of deep peace came down and covered me— and someone stood beside me—someone who took me gently by the arm and led me down the hill and back to my room. I never felt their touch, really. I only felt their presence and a deep and abiding peace—a peace such as I had never before known.

I vaguely remember retiring. I remember arising early—packing my suitcase—going to the station—getting a ticket—boarding a bus and traveling along without having to take any thought of how, or when, or even why. It was as though I had no power of volition—as though someone else, or something else, a higher force was arranging things for me, taking complete charge. I was being moved—not moving.

Then quite suddenly I was wide awake! It was the middle of the afternoon! I was on a bus! Traveling somewhere! But where? Where was I? And where was I going? It was like waking from a deep sleep in a strange place and searching desperately for one's bearings. I remembered clearly only the hilltop, the sunset—my pledge. But where was I? And where was I going?

"It's quite all right, Christine. Don't be alarmed. You're on your way to Los Angeles!"

I didn't hear the words with my ears. Rather were they poured into my being. And I sank back into my seat to marvel at the wonder of it.

Los Angeles was the last place on the face of the earth I intended to go. I had visited there several years before. I had had no reason for remaining the first time, and certainly knew of no reason now for going there. Then I realized that the dedication of my life had been accepted for the choice had not been mine. I would have preferred remaining in Yuma, in fact, had intended to if I could have found employment. Phoenix would have been my second choice—but Los Angeles—never!

I knew, with all the intelligence that I possessed, that I had been placed on that bus. The choice had not been mine, therefore, there must be a deep purpose for it.

That was all I knew. But that was enough. Just to be sure that higher power was taking a hand in my life was a joy beyond measure. It gave me a warm feeling of homecoming after a lifetime of wandering in a strange land. If my welcome was not with a brass band and rolled out carpets I still had no complaints. And the song of gratitude I had been cultivating since I had awakened to the realization of my selfishness—that singing song of glory that banished the darkness, the loneliness, the desperate despair, was increasing in my soul. It was enough.

It was more than enough though I had only seven dollars in my purse when I arrived, and though I had to spend five of it for a dingy little room crawling with cockroaches and bedbugs. How could I complain, I who had so much.

IV.

THE OFFERING OF A BROKEN-HEART

I arose from that defiled bed after that first night completely refreshed. I felt as though I had been bathed in dew and dried with rose petals. I was tingling with breathless anticipation. The very air throbbed with an alert eagerness. I was not an adventuress, but certainly was on my greatest adventure. The atmosphere was pregnant with promise. I felt as though I was being borne along on wings of light.

At the very first place I went I received employment. It was only a filing clerk job, but it would keep me until I found my bearings, or knew why I had been brought to Los Angeles.

Yes, that job would keep me, if only I could keep it. How I was going to live on one dollar and a half for two full weeks, not to mention room rent for the second week, was still unsolved. Yet the strangest part of the whole situation was that I felt perfectly at ease. I felt as though I had not a care in the world. I had no misgivings and no fears.

Perhaps the lesson I had learned before arriving in Yuma had helped to prepare me to meet startling circumstances without fear. At least the pledge I had given in the desert was something I could not go back on. That pledge had been woven out of the very fibres of my life and could not be put aside. I had pledged myself never to complain at anything, no matter what happened, or didn't happen. I had dedicated my life with a very solemn promise that I could not break.

And then I learned something very important. I learned that every lesson received must needs be followed by a test, for it is only as we pass the tests that destiny is satisfied.

I had made a pledge. Would I keep it? How sincere was I in my oath of dedication. I knew then, with a sure knowing, that unless I abided by my covenant I could not be trusted, nor could I be permitted to go on to greater heights—greater lessons—greater tests, perhaps. From somewhere I seemed to recall a phrase: "He must be tested and tried in all things." I had no idea where I had heard it, or even if I had ever actually heard it. But the thought took hold and added a meaning to the miserable room I occupied. Then for some inexplicable reason I hoped those tests would come fast and furious. Perhaps I was hoping to take in the whole gigantic life-time of living in one tremendous gulp. I didn't stop to realize that medicine given in small doses can be very helpful, but taken by the bottleful can be very deadly

I was consciously aware of my promise to "be thankful in all things—whatever came." And the pledge never to complain again. It was a big order I had cut out for myself. Now I had to make good on it. If I were to die I would live to the very last moment, with the very last breath, and the last flicker of intelligence, fully, intensively, completely, and gratefully—if possible. No more half-dead, whimpering existence for me. If I were meant to starve I was determined to enjoy starving. I would analyze it—every murderous pang of it. I would check its every action, and live above my reactions. I would observe the process with as much detachment as any modern scientist in his painstaking research. And when it was finished I would fully comprehend the experience to its last flickering pulse-beat. If I were to die of cancer, I, again, would understand it thoroughly before I finished with it—or rather, it finished me. I was going to learn to feel with an alert intensity of feeling that would demand of every experience everything it could possibly offer. I was determined to comprehend every minutest happening in my life — to live every vital breath to its fullest capacity. No moment was ever going to pass me by without yielding a measure of tribute.

Ronnie's going had taught me to gather the intense, exquisite torture of heartbreak and sorrow into the sacred crucible of my heart, and there to learn to triumph over them. It was that very experience of heartbreak that had equipped me for living. Ronnie had always had that inner equipment. I had had to begin to develop it by sheer will power and stupendous courage.

It would have been so much easier to have continued wallowing in my self-pity—to have gone on weeping over myself in my grim misfortune as other men were returning to their wives and sweethearts. I could have gone on in my bitterness, growing more hard and ugly in my blind resentment as I developed an intense hatred against life and destiny because I could have talked myself into believing that I alone was called to suffer —that none had ever suffered as I suffered. I could have dried up in my soul and wallowed in my deep, stifling self-pity—that is—if Ronnie had not been Ronnie. I get all weak and trembly, even now, when I realize how very near I came to failing—and probably would have, but for the grace of God.

Those who claim to have suffered more than anyone else has ever suffered have not yet learned the meaning of suffering. Whatever they have been called to endure has borne no fruits, been as wasted, as barren, as empty and void and meaningless as the tragic ordeal of giving birth to a still-born child, for the experience remains unglorified. All suffering, great or small, like the crucifixion, was meant to be transmuted into living, everlasting glory. It can be. Even being the mother of a still-born child can bring a benediction of such hallowed purification of soul, such infinite tenderness and understanding with it, that the experience can open wide the very portals of continued advancement. It is when man realizes the purpose of suffering and utilizes its power that all suffering will end. It will be then that man will come into his full dominion and have complete power to subdue the earth and all things and all conditions upon it. It will be then that the glorious privilege of suffering, the divine power of it, the sacred, breath-taking essence and wonder of it will be revealed. I find myself awed and overwhelmed by the unutterable glory of its hidden power. Any suffering, any pain, disappointment, heartbreak or even fear, when accepted with the true prayer of: 'Thy will be done" can be instantly transmuted into unlimited power.

Yea, "Come unto me, all you who labor and are heavy laden and I will give you rest." (Give me your burdens) "and take my yoke upon you, for my yoke is easy and my burden is light."

And: "The only sacrifice acceptable henceforth is the sacrifice of a broken heart and a contrite spirit."

As the broken heart, the sorrow, the pain, the

suffering, the burden of any mortal experience is offered to Him with the sincere prayer of: "Thy will be done"—and I mean offered without reservation, but with a complete letting go, the sacrificed burden can be exchanged for the yoke of love and a burden of complete enfolding light and glory and happiness and eternal power—power to overcome all things. This is the power of true dominion in all its divine majesty.

Perhaps because of Ronnie's greatness I had been touched with that awakening vision and made to realize that I was mourning over myself, Christine Mercie. It was not Ronnie I was weeping for, really. As I awoke to my miserable, groveling selfishness I was ashamed. Deeply ashamed.

It was such sorrows as these that had made Ronnie great. Every difficulty of his life had been made to yield its sacred essence and had become a building block in the structure of his soul.

How could I grieve over my lot with such knowledge? How could any outside condition leave me complaining wtih dismay? God had touched my understanding, and in that touch I was bequeathed a greater responsibility.

V.

THROUGH THE TUNNEL

So it was that my first day at work ended—
and my second—and my third—and I was walking
through the Third street tunnel to return to my
crawling room, for by now the nits or eggs,
of the bugs I had killed, were beginning to hatch
and I had no more disinfectant—and no money
to purchase any.

I was going thröugh the Third street tunnel
because my job was on Spring street and my
room was on West Third and Figueroa.

I still had ten cents in my purse. I still walked
with head held high and my jaunty little suit worn
with a new dash of sparkling rhythm. It seemed
to sense that there was something extra special
in the air. But perhaps it was but reflecting the
hidden joy that kept gurgling up with such per-
sistent, unquenchable singing from deep within my
heart.

I was quite aware that the song of triumph was
vibrating with a new note of ecstacy and my feet
scarcely touched the grimy, dust-laden, narrow,
dingy walk crowding itself along the tunnel wall.

41

The air was heavy with the fumes of evening traf-
fic. The place was dark, almost suffocating, but
I didn't notice its dreariness. It was an isle of
glory to me that evening, though I could give no
logical reason for it being so, nor for the extra
gladness singing a melody of ecstacy in my heart.
I was only aware that the melody was more joyous, more breathtakingly buoyant than usual. It
was quite beyond understanding, or logic. But
then, logic often drives men crazy. Besides, how
could my mind analyze the things my heart felt?

There is an inner intelligence higher than mortal
intellect, greater than logic, beyond thought,
higher than physical understanding, yet more real
than all. It is more than intuition, or faith, or
joy, or gladness. It is all of these and yet reaches
even beyond them all. It is the inner essence of
life itself.

I had contacted that singing song in the center
of my soul when I had offered up my broken heart.
I did not know at the time that only the offering
of a broken heart could bring a reward so great.
In fact, I had never realized that there was anything in existence so utterly, completely beautiful.

I was beginning to feel that if one great heartbreak could bring such a glorious song of sheer
ecstasy when offered upon the altars of acceptance
then I would be willing to have it broken many
times. In fact I would be willing to have it ground

into fine dust. Then I knew the answer. It is the complete offering of a broken heart that has the power to transmute all darkness into light. It is only through a broken heart that the pure love of God can come forth and it is that singing love that is the joy and the power and the triumphant ecstatic song awakened in the soul of man.

And so my soul sang as I winged my way through the tunnel, for it seemed that my feet scarcely touched the ground, so great was the joyous melody singing in my heart. It was a song of gladness, a song of adoration, of praise, of rejoicing, of love so deep and pure that everything seemed transformed by it. There was no ugliness in existence. It was the perfect love that banished all fear. It seemed to blend as one with the entire universe, the infinite, and all existing things. It was pure, singing glory.

The song seemed to increase in tempo as I proceeded through the tunnel. It was a vibration that suddenly seemed to turn into words. Not words I heard with my ears, but a deep inner voice of complete knowing—spoken without words; "Christine," it commanded gently, lovingly: "Now go and find a nice apartment."

I stopped dead in my tracks. If the tunnel had caved in on me I could not have been more surprised. I wheeled around, headed back toward Broadway, never doubting for an instant. How

I was to get an apartment in Los Angeles, of all places on the earth, in the busiest season of the year, and with one thin little dime in my pocket troubled me not at all. I was only conscious of being taken out of my bug-ridden room with four days to spare. I could have shouted with the very joy of it. There were no enclosing walls to that tunnel, no sealed roof overhead. I was walking in the very highest heaven.

I took ten or fifteen steps back toward the center of the city when I heard, "Don't go back. Turn around and go on through the tunnel."

Then, for the second time, I stopped short and wheeling around again went on toward Figueroa street.

But I never reached Figueroa. I was turned at Flower street, directed, propelled, call it what you like—I only know that I walked past many apartment buildings, past several hotels—and without stopping at any one of them, or even giving them a questioning glance, I continued on. At last I stood upon the threshold of the most luxurious apartment building in the area. And without hesitating an instant went up to the desk, above which hung the sign: ALL RENTS MUST BE PAID IN ADVANCE. And I did not see it. How I could have missed seeing it I cannot imagine. There it was, as big as life and standing out as prominent as a sore thumb. I can't imagine what I would have done if I had seen it. I might have folded up right then and there. I don't know. I can't even imagine.

"Have you a vacant apartment?" I asked the woman sitting behind the desk, and directly under that awesome sign that I didn't see. There had been no vacancy sign posted on the outside or within to denote such a possibility of an empty apartment. Ordinarily my very assumption would have been laughable and fantastic.

But as I spoke another gracious little lady, with white hair and an angel's face, stepped out of the inner office.

"Yes," she smiled brightly as she looked me over; "I have an available apartment, which is most unusual for this locality and for this time of the year. It was just re-painted today and isn't quite dry—but you will only need to be careful for this evening."

She seemed to know that I was going to move in then. I wondered how she knew.

She entered the elevator with me, and taking me up to the top floor, conducted me along a deep, rugged, beautiful hallway to a door with a minia-ture brass knocker upon it which seemed to con-tain a very special welcome, especially since none of the other doors had any.

The first thing I noticed, as we entered, was the

wide window which revealed a view that took my breath away.

"It's fairy land!" I cried. "It's pure magic! It's beautiful!"

The large neon Pegasus, on top of the Mobilgas building, was winging its flaming flight across the skies. The last dazzling glory of the sunset still lingered with a warm caress, a benediction, a reminder of another sunset—and a whispering promise of things to come. Then while I looked the street lights came on, sparkling like a string of diamonds encircling a lady's throat, and just at that moment the crowning glory of all burst into view as the rainbow lights flooded into living wonder on the top of the high, tiered black and gold Richfield building. Its spired tower reached up its flaming tip into the evening sky. My eyes took in the dignity of the beautiful, tiled pyramid of the library dome as it stood mysterious and silent against the dusk. And one by one a million lights blinked on in twinkling delight. It was like a scene from another world yet so close it took my breath away.

Like an excited child I tore myself away from the first window to turn to the second one, just as large, but facing another direction, with another fairyland of twinkling lights.

At last I turned from the windows to look over the apartment. It was a dream fulfilled. It was not new, but fresh with paint, spotlessly immaculate, cozy with a welcoming warmth of homecoming and magically inviting. It had everything—two long mirrors to check the hem of one's dress—a living room, a bed room, a dressing room, a bath and kitchen and a convenient little hallway, all its own.

"This will cost more a month than I earn," I thought. Yet with the thought was the absolute knowledge that I was to have that apartment.

"How much is it?" I at last ventured.

The woman looked at me and smiled softly, "You may have it for fifty dollars a month. I rent it for more, but I would like to have you in my building. You see, I own it, and I just happened to stop by for a few minutes tonight. I don't live here.

"Perhaps I came just to meet you," she said contemplatively.

"I must have this apartment," I said; "And it is so gracious of you to offer it to me for only fifty dollars—but I just arrived in Los Angeles three days ago and haven't any money to pay down. I have work and could pay you in a couple of weeks. I paid for a room over the corner of Figueroa and Third street but it is crawling with roaches and I can't possibly stay there." I stated it as though it was the most commonplace thing in the world to go apartment seeking without money.

"Of course you can't stay there," she agreed.

"I would be glad to let you keep my hand-tooled leather bag and my bracelet and brooch set as security. I have never been in such a position in my life before," I laughed.

"I am sure you haven't. It is a new experience for both of us," she smiled; "We should become good friends."

And that was it! The apartment was mine! It was mine! I couldn't believe it! I was going to leave the bugs and the darkness and the filth! I had passed my test! If I could have shouted aloud with all my capacity it would never have been loud enough to express my joy and gratitude. I had not resented the misery of that unclean room. I had not complained. I had truly been thankful! And now! A paradise—a hundred-fold better had been added unto me.

Mrs. Wilcox, for that was the owner's name, insisted that I keep my bag, but I assured her that I had no need of it. Why carry a bag if there is no money to go in it? At that we both laughed.

Mrs. Wilcox didn't come to the building too often. However, she did come the day my rent was to be paid, and to return my bag. I think she came herself so that the clerk would not know that I had lived there for two full weeks without paying a cent or that I was renting an apartment she could easily have got eighty-five dollars for, for only fifty.

As she handed me my receipt, Mrs. Wilcox smiled again her warm, glowing, heavenly smile and said, "You were led here, weren't you?"

"Yes. I was," I answered. And I told her how it happened.

"I knew you were brought to me when I saw you. I knew that I had come in that evening just to meet you. I feel so humble and so grateful when I am called to play a small part in the hands of destiny."

My eyes filled with tears of gratitude and the singing song of glory must have been heard all over that whole, wonderful building.

What I lived on for those two weeks was another miracle, a very beautiful miracle.

I had no sooner got my suitcase into that apartment than again I heard that inner voice of minute instruction telling me how to obtain food. You may believe that I thought of it all by myself. I didn't. I would never have thought of it because it was something beyond my knowledge. I did not know that Karl Morgan, a childhood acquaintance of mine, was a supervisor at the Carnation Creamery Company. I did know that Karl had moved to California several years before. But

I did not know he was in Los Angeles, nor what his work was.

But I was told: "Christine, Karl Morgan is a supervisor at the Carnation Creamery. Call him up. Tell him you just got settled and would like to order two quarts of milk, delivered every other day, some cottage cheese, a dozen eggs as often as you need them, and a bottle of half-and-half, which is half cream and half milk."

I used my precious little dime to call the Carnation Creamery and asked for Karl Morgan. And marvel of marvels! He was in! Or was it? To me it was as great a miracle as the feeding of the five thousand. Their meal was only to appease the hunger. Mine was a matter of life and death— of starvation or living.

Karl and I had a wonderful chat. He sounded really glad to hear me. And I was almost over-whelmed with the wonder of it all. After discussing many things I gave my order.

"I think the driver for your route calls in the morning, early. Wait while I check."

I waited with one foot teetering in heaven and the other balanced on a silver cloud.

In a few minutes came his voice, "Christine, the driver will be at your door at eight in the morning. Will that be all right?"

'Just perfect," I answered, for only I knew how

perfect. I would have breakfast before going to work.

"And Christine," he continued; "I will fill out the application blank and o.k. it so it can be sent right on through without any delay.

"And, by-the-way, when can you come and have dinner with us? I'd like you to meet my wife. She's wonderful. Could you come Monday?"

I had no bus fare so I said, "Not Monday, Karl, not until the nineteenth. That's two weeks off. I have a lot of business to attend to besides getting settled."

"That will be wonderful! I'll be seeing you then. Say, I'm surely glad I happened to come in this evening for a few minutes."

"Aren't you always in, in the evening?" I asked, while little goose pimples began keeling summer-saults up and down my spine.

"I've been here for nine years and this is the first time I have ever come to the office in the evening," he laughed.

And that was that. I didn't even know until sometime later that it was necessary to have a bank account, plus references and several other requirements, I didn't possess, in order to have a milk man deliver dairy products to the door. But forever and forever I shall be grateful for the wonderful blessing it gave.

The next morning as I was walking to work, a

woman standing with several others waiting for a bus, dropped her bag on the sidewalk. Coins rolled every-which-way. We all began helping her to pick them up. We had just unloaded our collections when the bus came and all who had been standing there boarded it. I turned down the street on my way to work when I saw a fifty-cent piece leaning against the light post. I picked it up, turned hastily back toward the departing bus. It was already crossing the intersection at the other corner. Fifty cents and no owner.

With that coin I bought two loaves of day-old bread at half price and some fresh dates. And from there on I lived like a princess in my castle above the clouds. It could easily be said, "And I lived happily ever-after." But the story is only beginning.

VI.

THE VEIL OF UNBELIEF

I had been working for several months, had received two very important promotions—and had made many friends. The song of glory singing in my soul was like a magnet, attracting others to me. I had grown so terribly morbid, so dark in my thinking and self-pity, in the east, that I had become repellent and only those still visited me who were bound by loyalty or were endowed with a greater fortitude than most.

This singing song of glory, that was becoming a very part of me, was a power of light that reached out in warmth to enfold a world. There were moments when I actually felt that the world could come and warm itself at the sacred fires burning in my soul. And there were many more times when I am sure that those I contacted in my work felt it also.

There were, of course, those who resented me. They resented anyone being so extremely happy, not that I was emphasizing the fact or trying to flaunt it. It was only that I could not possibly contain it all and it would splash out in sheer, ecstatic living.

Miss Barker resented it greatly. Miss Barker did not know how to be happy. She wouldn't have known how to handle it if it had come to her in hunks big as the world. Part of her happiness was the ability to be extremely unhappy. And it was Miss Barker who remarked, "What chance do the rest of us have against Christine?"

"What do you mean?" asked little Martha innocently.

"What do I mean? Why I'm surprised at you, Martha. Christine isn't like the rest of us. She doesn't have to work for a living. Christine has never had anything but success and happiness in her whole life. She was born with a silver spoon in her mouth, a college degree in her crib, a gilt-edge guaranteed success affidavit in her hand, a million dollars in her bootie."

"Wow!" I thought; "even the scars must have disappeared." And instead of resenting her remark and her attitude I felt as if I stood on sacred, but hard-earned, ground.

I had more difficulty with the men. They wanted to take hold of that inner something that I possessed. I had to veil the stardust in my eyes, muffle the song in my heart, conceal the breathtaking, glorious gratitude in my soul or they would, almost without exception, unconsciously start grab-

bing at me. I knew it was not me they desired. It
was that singing, illusive light of glory. But they
understood it not at all. I had to be careful. Not
only to guard myself, but also to guard them. Age
seemed to make no difference — and marriage
seemed no hindrance at all to most of them. It
wasn't that they didn't love their wives, or that
they were unhappily married. Then suddenly I
didn't believe that it was diamonds people wished
to possess particularly, it was the glitter they desired to own—that sparkling, shining, inner light.

I realized fully that it was not me they wanted.
It was the sparkling, intangible light, the elusive
song, the melody of gladness and rapture.

Of course it was impossible for me to explain
that they could own it only as they themselves
developed it from within. Then, and only then,
could they own that which they were grabbing
at me for.

Then there was little Martha, plain lovable little
Martha who could never resent anyone, nor comprehend how Miss Barker felt. Martha was timid,
unnoticed, unexciting. I once wondered how they
even remembered to give her a pay check, not because she wasn't efficient, but because she was
completely unobtrusive. She was just a little cog
in the wheels of the office. But it was Martha to
whom I shall be forever grateful.

I came upon her in the women's lounge, at

lunch time, reading the last page of a book. She looked up with a far-away expression in her eyes as I entered and whispered in an awed undertone, "It's not possible! It simply isn't possible!"

"What isn't possible?" I asked, not that she was talking to me. She wasn't. She was just talking to herself.

"Why—this book. All of it! It's like nothing else I've ever read in my life. My aunt told me to get it from the library—But listen to this little typewritten note stuck in here at the end: 'Anna-lee Skarin, the author of this book, disappeared from her room while visiting friends in June, 1951. She has not been seen or heard from since. Her clothes were left in the closet. Her car in the yard.'"

"Probably kidnapped—or wandered away. Or may have been seeking publicity," I suggested.

"No. I don't think so. If one is seeking publicity he, or she, would surely have to show up to seek its reward. It isn't the sort of book such a person as that would write. Neither could such a one be kidnapped—or—just disappear. Here, Christine, take it home with you tonight and glance through it. I have to have dinner with the relatives this evening. But be sure and bring it back to me in the morning. I must read it again."

"I'd love to read it," I said, thinking I was doing her a favor.

I doing her a favor?

That book was the most tremendous thing that had ever come into my hands. It reached inside of me and taking hold of my soul took it out of my body and stood it up before my eyes in all its pristine, glittering splendor as it soared forth from the very throne of God to fulfill its glorified destiny— a destiny far beyond the ken of mortal understanding. It rolled back the curtains of existence and revealed the glorified drama of life —the past, the present, the future—the eternal, NOW and forevermore, in a magic touch of breathtaking power.

To put it mildly, Annalee Skarin's book, *Ye Are Gods*, "knocked me for a loop," even as it had Martha. I never went to bed that night. I'd read, then walk the floor in flames of ecstasy— and then return to read some more—and yet some more.

"How could such a book be written!" I thought. "And how could one bear to read it," for it was blinding in the revelation it contained. Later I learned that Annalee Skarin felt exactly that way about it as she wrote it.

I knew what Martha meant when she said she had to have the book back so she could read it again. I wanted so to keep it another day—to spend another night reading it, but Martha would be waiting for it.

I was re-reading parts of it even while I dressed for work.

It was no longer necessary for me to walk through the Third street tunnel on my way to and from work, but often I went out of my way to go through it. I always felt as though there was a key in that tunnel which should be revealed. I used to walk through it watching moving figures at the far end floating along like tiny shadows silhouetted in an unreal way against the wall. I guess that was it. The tunnel seemed, in some vague way, to be a connecting passage between the real and the unreal—or between the possible, shall I say, and the impossible.

Perhaps I felt that way about it because it was in that tunnel I received such a great lift—for I was lifted from a little bug infested room into an apartment of utter beauty.

So it was on this morning, after a sleepless night, I felt that only a trip through the tunnel could find a small expression of the deep feelings and thoughts that book had stirred up in me.

I left a little early to give myself plenty of time to go through the tunnel without hurrying too fast. I knew people were dismayed and depressed at the necessity of going through it. I was elated. I loved it. There could not have been any possible reason for me feeling as I did about it except the thing I had experienced just after my arrival in the city. Yet when my feet seemed to be extra light I usually took the time to go through it.

I was about one third of the way through, going toward Hill street, when a truck came roaring down upon me, stirring up the dust. A cinder, a stone, a hunk of dirt flew into my eye with sting-ing agony. I closed my eyes momentarily as I ploughed blindly on.

And then in an instant the pain was gone. As suddenly as it had come it was gone. I opened my eyes in relief—

I was not in the tunnel! I spun around to look behind me for it! It just wasn't!

I was in a great hall! It was filled with light —exquisite, living light, brilliant, quiet, with an "out-of-this-world" peace about it. What had happened I couldn't imagine. A moment before I had been in that tunnel that stretched for three long city blocks between Hope and Hill streets. Now I was in a place I had never before been in. I looked down at myself. I was clothed as I had been—my bag was in my hand—and the book —Annalee Skarin's precious book, *Ye Are Gods*, was still tucked safely under my arm.

I glanced up to see someone coming toward me—someone—and then a cry of joy escaped my lips, "Oh, Ronnie! Ronnie! Darling, I'm dead! I'm dead! How wonderful! How wonderful!"

"No, Christine, you are not dead. You are very much alive!"

"Yes, I know—but the truck—it must have hit me—"

"No, the truck never touched you, dear," and he smiled in such a tender, amused way, and with such gentle love I had to shake the tears out of my eyes.

"Tell me about it!" I cried; "Oh, Ronnie, tell me all about it."

"First give me the book. It must be returned to Martha. She is waiting for it—and it is what she needs."

"Then the book IS true! IT IS true! I knew it had to be! I knew it!" I thrilled exultantly.

"Yes, Christine, it is true. That book was written by the very finger of God. All of the forces of evil have risen to fight it—to destroy the sacred message it contains. All the forces of darkness are seeking to submerge it. But you never doubted it. How wonderful of you, Christine! It is your not doubting that has made you become a part of it. Later you will meet Annalee and she will assist you in writing the things that are yours to tell."

"How marvelous!" I exclaimed. "How very marvelous! I would rather meet Annalee Skarin than anyone else I can think of, except you, Ronnie."

"My Christine, my precious Christine. How very proud I am of you."

"You proud of me?" I gasped in surprise.

"Of course, my dear! You've overcome the darkness—and when you spoke to me across the desert that night the whole universe gave ear. Your words will live forever. My precious, Christine."

"Then I can stay? We can go on together?" I cried eagerly. For from the beginning I had had an inner feeling that I was going to have to return to earth, or to the daily routine of mortal living.

"Not yet, Christine. Not yet. You and I belong—but for a little while our assignments will be on different planes. You still have your body."

"I do?" I asked surprised. "Then what am I doing here? How did I get here?"

"You rent the veil of unbelief! But come, dear! They are waiting for you."

"Who?"

"The great Brotherhood of Light — The Assembly, or Church of the Firstborn — The Noble and great ones whom God has reserved unto Himself, which the world knows not of — the glorious Sons of God — those who have truly been born again, not of words and speeches and theories—but of the Spirit of the Almighty."

Ronnie took me to a great door which opened at our approach.

"Enter, darling. I shall see you again."

I reached out my hand to stop him, but he was already moving away. And immediately I was ushered into the great assembly.

The place, room, temple, assembly room, whatever it is called, was like nothing I had ever beheld. It was immense in its unbelievable expanse and majesty. I know the description is trite and meaningless, but there are no words in any language to describe it.

There was music—music that vibrated to the song that had been developing in my soul, only more glorious, more triumphant, more divine. My melody was but a faint awakening echo of that heavenly song of universal triumph. It wasn't just sound. There were no words with it. It was a vibration of power so alive, so glorified it could be felt and seen. It was light—the great light of Almighty God as it flowed out from the very bosom of eternity to create, to redeem, to make alive, to uplift, and exalt and glorify. It was the great divine Light of Christ, the very power of existence and creation and life.

I had called that song the song of gratitude. It was that. It had been my "Thank You" prayer of such loving devotion, such deep gratitude that every blessing had multiplied an hundred-fold almost automatically. As my gratitude had increased my blessings increased. It was the complete fulfillment of multiplying and replenishing every blessing on the earth. It was more, it was the power that would transmute tragedy into joy, failure into success, loss into blessings—darkness into Light. The law of "thanks-giving" and gratitude is the divine law of multiplication. It is the law of bringing-forth, of creation, of increase. As it poured into my being in its complete fullness I realized the purpose and the power of such infinite harmony. It is a song of love and devotion, of praise and exaltation, of gratitude and thanks that can clothe one in complete glory. It is the Celestial symphony of the Universe. It is the "New Song" that is not learned in words, but which is felt and released from the very center of the soul. It is divine, perfected love. It is developed from within by being grateful for every little blessing received—and those little blessings begin to multiply.

That stupendous room, if it can possibly be called by such a name, was circular in its immense dimension of breathtaking grandeur. There were rows upon rows of individuals seated within the ever-expanding circle. Only the center, twenty-foot space, was open and unoccupied, except for one person. The floor seemed to be of glass, or pure crystal, or perhaps one large, perfect diamond, for it reflected lights and colors with sparkling brilliance.

The individual standing in the center welcomed

me forward, down one of the many aisles that led
from the great doors in the outer walls to the center
of the assembly room, or to that twenty-foot circular, open space. It is most difficult to give descrip-
tions for no language of the earth has the power
of expression needed to impart the full information
of Celestial grandeur.

All I can say is that the individual presiding
over that particular assembly was glory personi-
fied. Love and light seemed actually to flow
from his being, his robes, his eyes, his very
finger tips. I could not stand in such a place, before such hallowed ones. I sank down upon my
knees and bowed my head in profound reverence
washed in tears.

"Arise, Christine! And welcome! We have been
waiting for you, dear sister!" Then it was as
though I heard, or rather felt, every voice in that
vast assembly whisper softly and with such infinite
tender love, "Welcome, dear sister." I had the
feeling suddenly as though I knew each and every
individual in that divine assembly, as though I
were clasping their hands and they mine. Every
trace of self-consciousness vanished and I stood
straight, while a great light seemed to pour itself
over me and through me.

"The whole heavens are rejoicing over you,
Christine, for you have passed through the veil of
unbelief."

"The veil of unbelief?" I repeated, for I recalled Ronnie saying the same thing, and I desired
to know the meaning of the words.

"Yes, the veil of unbelief. It is only this veil of
unbelief that shuts mankind out from us.

"That veil has grown more solid than steel, or
concrete, or marble, or any physical substance
in existence. Its density has increased with the
ages. It is built from the very hardness of men's
hearts, which hardness is harder than any other
substance in the entire universe. It is re-inforced
with the blindness of their minds and is woven
of gross wickedness, for a completely hardened
heart is one of the most wicked conditions possible
to attain. It is often caused by minds that *will
not* see. This condition does not belong just to
criminals, often their hearts are more softened
than one who considers himself a saint. To be
able to believe all things makes all things possible.

"The overcoming of unbelief is accomplished
most readily by those who will offer their broken
hearts upon the altar of God, without rebellion,
bitterness or self-pity for it must be offered with
a love and devotion that truly desires God's will
tc be accomplished above everything else. Therefore, it becomes a dedication of thanks, or praise,
or divine love that can melt the heart completely
and thus the veil can be rent by any on the earth
who only perfect the gift of divine love. It is

this offering of a broken heart, mingled with melting, inner tenderness that overcomes the unbelief and can rend the veil."

"Millions on the earth are suffering from heartbreak," I ventured.

"Yes, Christine, but they are mis-using their greatest instrument of divine glory. Instead of offering their heartbreak to God in praise and thanksgiving for the very power it contains, and truly desiring the heartbreak to continue, if it be His will, they harden their hearts even more, thus increasing the scales upon their eyes, the darkness in their souls and the great veil becomes continually more impenetrable.

"Glory to those who can rend this veil! Glory be to them!" And I felt it echoed and breathed out in infinite love by the multitude.

"We cannot rend that veil. It is constructed of mortal vibrations and only man can rend it. Each individual must rend it for himself. And each individual who does rend it makes it easier for those who follow. That is why the heavens rejoice over you, Christine. You finally took your heartbreak and offered it to God without restrictions, and the very power and weight of your burden, when thus transmuted could rend the veil for you. You let your heart become softened, instead of hardened by the experience, therefore you could learn to believe, without question, without doubt.

It is heartbreak that causes the hard heart to crack, or open—and that opening can be used for such unspeakable power and advancement as is overwhelming in its full manifestation—or that opening can be immediately reinforced, thus sealing in the sorrow and shriveling the very fibres of the soul. It is up to each individual how he reacts to it. The unspeakable power of God can be his to use, or the bitterness of hell can enfold him forever in its darkness.

"How beautiful! How beautiful it is to know such things!" I cried, filled with the marvel and the wonder of the very simplicity of it.

"Yes, it is beautiful! And for you, Christine, the veil is gone forever. You can pass to and fro as the occasion requires.

"There is yet a great work for you to do upon the earth. You are needed there in your tangible, mortal form. Your work will be varied according to the needs of men. You will also be privileged to write a partial account of your experience, the first to be given such an assignment. If you need help, Annalee will help you."

He ceased speaking and I glanced at the multitude surrounding me. I felt their love pouring out to me. I felt that I knew each and every one of them—that our hearts blended as one, in complete, everlasting unity. And I was sure that they each knew me, perhaps better than I knew them.

They had watched my progress, had given me of their strength, had directed my way as I had responded to their help.

How one in mortal body could endure the grandeur of the things that were mine to experience I do not know unless my body was quickened by the Spirit of God.

These great ones were clothed, but not in cloth —in pure, spun light. It was glorified Light, blazing in splendor—living, eternal Light.

There were both men and women. All were as one in the great love they sent out to enfold all, the earth, mankind, the universe.

And the vibration of that song that had been developing in my heart was their song—It was the "NEW SONG"—the very song of God that only the righteous can learn. It had only been a faint echo in my soul, yet that faint echo had become a living power of fulfillment. Then I realized the song is always there, going forth. It is the pure vibration of gratitude and love and praise and pure devotion. And when any heart opens, even a tiny crack to permit it to enter, it helps to open the soul for greater things.

It is when this precious melody of love becomes the living essence of one's being that its power begins to be made manifest. It is the vibration of spontaneous, glorified life itself. It is for all mankind to express and those who only will de-

velop the "ears to hear," which mean the power
to FEEL, that song will become a power of ever
increasing strength. Each individual who develops
the power to hear it has the ability to multiply
its volume and send it on—out to touch the
burdened hearts of a weary world. That song is
a prayer, a spontaneous prayer, pure and undefiled.
It is not a "God, give me—" prayer. And he who
sings that song in his soul shall be made glorious.
It is a song of great gratitude, born of love. "He
who is thankful in all things shall be made glorious, and the things of this earth shall be added
unto him an hundred-fold; yea, more."

It was that inner song of praise that had lifted
me from the bug-ridden room into one a hundred-
fold better. And as one continues to praise and
worship and adore that hundred-fold is increased
and continues to increase—forever.

Yet this power of increasing is not its full purpose. This power to multiply blessings is the
law upon which it operates.

Its purpose is to open or rather, melt the heart
that the veil of unbelief might be conquered. It
produces and develops a love so great all things
melt before it. It contains a love that forgets self
completely and with such infinite tenderness desires
only His will to be done. It perfects this complete
letting-go of all personal desires—and then only

can the individual become glorious—for that alone
IS His will.

It was then that I understood pain, suffering
and heartbreak in their true light—not as punishment sent by God, but as blessings, for in them
were contained the very keys of progress, Light,
power and complete dominion. In themselves they
were just what they appeared to be, unbearable
burdens, but when accepted and enfolded in the
faith and love of man they can be transmuted
into utter, eternal glory. Man has true dominion
over them, if he will but use it. They contain
the power that can turn darkness into light, poverty
into plenty, heartbreak into ecstasy, pain into
joy unspeakable. In man are the keys and the
power and the dominion to rule over them, to subdue them—to glorify them. Or to be destroyed
by them.

How simple it is when one understands. Truly
the "Mysteries of Godliness" are but the mysteries
of the great, simple truth of God's laws. It is
the understanding of these laws that is eternal
truth—the truth, which if used will make one
forever free.

VII.

THE DAY OF JUDGMENT

"Look close, Christine, and view the world," spoke the soft, penetrating voice of the glorified one taking charge of the assembly.

"The greatest drama of the universe is being enacted upon the world at the present time. It is the stage the whole Universe is watching, for the drama is nearly over, the climax draws near.

"Man is the crucible in which the powers of light and darkness are pouring their forces—for it is Judgment Day—not as it has been understood, but as it really is—not a day, according to man's thinking, but a period of time in which each man is judging himself. Truly Christ judgeth no man. Each man judgeth himself as being prepared and worthy to go on into the realms of light—or to be sent to lower, often inferior worlds, to progress slowly through the coming ages. Each man sets his own gauge—measures his own speed—makes his own choice. It is almost possible to predict the exact future of each individual, for the seeds they plant in their hearts,

and abide by, such will they reap. None need to
be told what each tree in an orchard will produce.
It is established from the very planting of the seed.

"Those who sow the wind must reap the whirl-
wind." "As they sow, so shall they reap."

"For some, the second death is all that is left,"
added the speaker.

"The second death!" I gasped. "Is there really
such a thing?"

"Oh yes. But look and you will understand
the great enfolding mercy of even that. Behold!"

And I looked down and beheld that the floor
was as a sea of glass, a telescope, a great lense,
I know not which, or how, or what—only I was
able to behold the whole earth—all of it—and
the inhabitants thereof. I saw the great forces of
light being poured out upon the earth from this
group, from other groups—from the very throne
of God, in ever increasing brilliance. It was being
poured out with increasing measure upon all flesh.

I saw that these great and mighty Sons of God,
these, who were gathered into the great Church
of the Firstborn, the divine Brotherhood of Light
were those who overcame WHILE IN THE FLESH.
This group inherit a far more exceeding place
and weight of glory than those, even, who just live
very good lives. Those who just live good lives
yet are overcome by the flesh will be disappointed
if they have been anticipating a great reward.

Unless one learns to fulfill the great laws of righteousness here, while in this life, he cannot be
exalted in the Celestial realms. Death does not
create a divine being or a celestial change in
anyone. It only reveals completely, to himself,
what he really is, his worthiness or unworthiness,
as the case may be. It is the complete unveiling
of himself to himself, and is often quite shocking.

As the light was poured out from the great, divine realms of God I saw many of the humble,
seeking ones lift up their heads with an inner
listening. I beheld this light begin to penetrate
their hearts, even as it had mine. I saw it warm
their souls as its righteousness began to increase
on the earth. I felt, rather than heard, that singing
song of everlasting thanksgiving and love touch
their hearts with its healing, awakening power,
and their own respond to its glory. I saw the
power of it, the breath taking wonder and majesty
of it. I felt its magnitude, its throbbing, everlasting thanksgiving and love touch their hearts with
its healing, awakening power, and their own respond to its glory. I saw the power of it, the
breath taking wonder and majesty of it. I felt
its magnitude, its throbbing, everlasting strength
and knew that it was these rays or vibrations of
living light that had brushed my cheek, penetrated
into the dark recesses of my mind, warmed my
soul, even as it was doing to countless others. By

keeping one's mind unsealed and open its influence can enter and grow. Thus each man is his own judge. He condemns himself with his blind, sealed, shut in, narrowed opinions, resentfulness, bitterness or hardness of heart, or he permits himself to pass on to a higher grade of advancement.

I beheld those in high places, and those in evil slums, and in the many ordinary paths of life begin to resist the light— the proud because it would dethrone their pride—the evil because they loved darkness rather than light. They were like the unclean things of earth that cannot bear the sunlight, but crawl under boards and stones and deep caverns to escape it.

There is no escape from the light as it is being poured out, except to lay hold upon the darkness —and then the darkness takes over—and from it there is no escape.

Those who have considered themselves the very sanctified of earth are fighting it harder than most others. This light is taking the usurped power of God and placing it back where it belongs—the great power that flows unrestricted between God and all mankind, unless blocked by the usurpation and bigotry of leaders. Those who have stood to block the flow of this power to all are being, or will be shortly shoved aside.

And I heard the ancient chant and saw the power of it: "God is thrusting the mighty from their seats, and exalting those of low degree." I saw those words come to life. I saw the Spirit of the Lord, as it was being poured out upon the earth, begin to crumble authorities, and nations as leaders and politicians and potentates sought to hold their posts. I saw them reach out with their blinded minds and draw the darkness to them as the only weapon with which they could fight. And thus, because of the hardness of their hearts and the blindness of their minds, they were seized with the very chains of hell. And the veil of unbelief grew more dense because of the great wickedness of the leaders. Thus they judged themselves as unworthy or unprepared for light, and rejecting it they were left unto themselves to begin to fight against the very power of God, and to persecute the Saints of the Most High. Thus they would be retarded by their pride for many ages, for pride is the greatest weapon of the powers of hell.

Pride is the false jewel, the counterfeit gem, worn as a diadem by those who are satisfied with the outward show of things. But he who wears this cheap counterfeit jewel has the seal of Lucifer upon his brow, and unless it is cast off the powers of darkness will claim the individual who wears it—for it is a seal. This pride is the chief weapon of the darkness. It fathers hate and jealousy, greed and falsehood and blinds the eyes of men. It hard·

ens their hearts and fortifies the veil of unbelief.

Then I beheld those—so very few—whose lives had been so evil, so filled with shame, so enfolded in darkness, so corrupt and wicked that when the great revelation came they pleaded for non-existence—the second death—for they could not bear the burden of their sins. For them there was no forgiveness because they had not sinned from ignorance or weakness, but from knowledge and strength, knowingly and wantonly. It was when their works had failed and the great shock of their wickedness stood fully revealed that they had to die for they could not possibly carry the unbearable burden of their crimes. Only spiritual death could bring relief for such great suffering as they had created. No soul could possibly go on existing and bear a burden so great. For them the second death was the greatest possible mercy. Only by it could the knowledge and the memory of their crimes be consumed, for only those reached this point who had not only sinned against themselves and against God, in every possible way, but had sinned against the human race—Had shed innocent blood and fought constantly to dethrone the Light and to exalt themselves in its stead. These were those who had deliberately ensnared the souls of men, who had brought untold misery and suffering and darkness upon the earth. To them it would be a great relief to die the second death—which death was often like physical death, slow and lingering—and torturous. To some it came by inches. To those who die this second death it is necessary to give up their ages of conscious existence, to release their individualities, their eons of development, their very souls, to be absorbed back as energy into the eternal fires of the great eternal Light—No longer a conscious entity—no longer —anything.

All others will be saved eventually—in some degree. But there are as many degrees of salvation as there are ideas of heaven in the minds of the millions of Christians.

It is a vain and stupid thing for men to go around shouting that they have been saved. Of course they have! So will all men be saved, except the sons of perdition, those who have merited only the second death, and they are very few. To be saved is no great credit to anyone. That is the gift Christ gave. No man really has to earn it. His only responsibility is to claim it, not to forfeit it.

But there are the exalted ones, these are the ones, who by their own efforts, by the development and use of love, the compassionate, tender, merciful love of Christ, have offered up their broken hearts and have gathered to themselves the Light in a vibrating melody of eternal power to subdue the earth, the evil conditions upon it and the darkness thereof. These are the ones who have "OVERCOME" and receiving the power of God, step forth with all things under their feet. This group is the Church of the Firstborn. They are gathered from every creed, from every nation, from the highways and the byways of life, from the cities and the hamlets, from the deserts and the mountains. They are gathered according to their power to rend the veil of unbelief. These are the ones who have learned the power of the broken heart, who, walking in contriteness of spirit and perfected love have overcome all things. They are unstained by the sins of the world. These are those who "Have purified themselves."

Those who have lived ordinary lives of goodness will get a high degree of glory and happiness, according to their merits.

But only those who *overcome all things in this life* are fully exalted.

This great judgment is as varied as are the individual lives of men. To each will be his own reward—his own place—his own heaven.

This great outpouring of the Spirit of the Lord is bringing all things to a speedy fruition. The time is being shortened by it. This great outpouring of the Spirit of the Lord as it is beginning to cover the earth, even as the waters cover the sea, is dynamic in its scope and in its results. It is being poured out upon all flesh, but all flesh

is not responding to its healing, purifying rays.
"Their sons and their daughters will prophesy,"
but their elders and their rulers will at first con-
demn them for it, and will do all manner of evil
to silence them.

In this great outpouring light there are no walls
to hide behind—no blinds to draw. The very souls
of men stand out, x-rayed against the background
of their lives—and their lives are x-rayed and
weighed against the background of their aims,
their desires, their weaknesses and their strength.
Weaknesses and errors can be enfolded in mercy,
while those who deliberately fight against the light
and truth of God, even as most are doing, by
pretending to be serving God, will find the judgment falls heavy. Through this light no one single
thing remains unknown, or unrevealed. None can
be hidden, cloaked or veiled from sight. None
are forgotten. None can escape.

As I stood there in that awesome interval looking
into the minds and hearts of men, yes, even into
the very depths of their souls, it was like seeing
with the "All-Seeing Eye" of the Almighty.

Those who were responding to the vibrations of
love and light, even in the least degree, were instantly noted. For them the great doors opened
wide. The great assembly of those mighty ones
poured out their love, inspiring, directing, assist-
ing in every possible way, giving constant help

and encouragement, though unseen. They poured out comfort and strength according to the individual's power to receive.

No one ever asks for help who is rejected, neglected, or unheard. Always as much help is bestowed as is possible to give under the individual circumstances, and the circumstances depend entirely on the receptivity and condition of the person needing help.

There are helpers always from that unseen side eagerly ready to assist any who sincerely seek and ask. The one requirement is that the asking be sincere. Only sincerity, deep and earnest can prepare any soul to receive help, or to use it if given. These great ones can only assist. They cannot do the work for another. That is the one impossible thing—even as one cannot die for another—or be born for another.

And there are also those helpers who are working on the earth who are still in physical form, who can be seen, but unrecognized by the great majority. But for everyone who sincerely reaches out for help, who seeks, or desires, or strives, help is sent. Sometimes it may be through an inspired thought entering the mind, a printed article, a book, a word, a sentence or a complete message given to the soul as a great revelation. Direction comes constantly to all who only open their minds and hearts to its continual flow.

The only ones who cannot be helped are those
who are sealed—either by believing that they already possess all light and all truth—or those who
are completely hardened by crime. No one in
mortality can possibly possess all the Light—if
he could he would no longer be mortal. But only
those who realize that they do not possess all the
light possible to receive are open to receive more,
and yet more.

As I comprehended the tender, constant care
that had been so freely given to me, my heart
melted completely into tears of deep, everlasting
gratitude.

I beheld the literal, breath taking, wondrous fulfillment of: "The meek shall inherit the earth" as
it began to unfold. I saw their meekness develop
and become powerful in its strength as the proud
and the haughty began to be cast from their high
and mighty seats.

I had a moment of great difficulty in adjusting
my mind to receive the knowledge that some of
the very proudest of all men were the leaders of
churches. As I beheld it I felt a great unspeakable shame come over me for them. So very, very
few who claimed to be the ambassadors, or rep-
resentatives of Christ had any Christ-like trait. I
bowed my head and wished with all my soul that
I could make up to God, in some way, for the
complete mockery of their empty service. They

would arise almost in mass to fight against the very Son of God if He appeared to rebuke them for usurping His power to glorify themselves. They were even shoving God aside and placing themselves up as His mouthpieces. They were "Blind Word of God, for it is most assuredly true that, leaders of the blind," the greatest tragedy of all.

But thank God all mankind is not blind. The meek and humble are responding more and more to the light—the eternal glory—the very voice, or "The Word of the Lord is Truth; and whatsoever is Truth, is Light; and whatsoever is Light, is Spirit, even the Spirit of Jesus Christ"—which Spirit is the great vibration of love and light and intelligence and power. It is the inner Light of God that is in the midst of all things. It is the inner light that is in the very center, or midst of all things that is being contacted by the great out-pouring light of heaven. It is the blending of these two lights that awakens one to service, to life, and glory and eventual perfection.

And so I viewed the commencement of the way of the meek and the beginning of the re-dedication of the earth to them. I watched them beginning to rise from their humble stations, as they were slowly, slowly being filled with light, according to their individual capacities. And the light which they received was the great Light, the Light of power, even the power of the Almighty.

Such is the beginning of the Day of Judgment. And such is its end.

The rest of what was given to me I cannot share. Even if I could, none would be able to comprehend except those who have already rent the veil of unbelief. And they already know.

And finally I was given the holy anointing and the words: "Christine, you are ordained with a holy calling to help spread the sacred Light. Give it to none who are unworthy lest it injure or consume them. This is what Christ meant when He commanded his apostles to let their peace return unto them whenever they contacted those who could not receive it, or who were unworthy.

"Give out the Light, Christine. Let it shine forth, but only to the degree that individuals are prepared to receive it lest too much at one time destroy.

"Tread carefully the sacred highway of the divine.

"Whenever there is a task too difficult, just call and help will come. The strength of all is back of each one. This is the power of unity, of true brotherhood in the Divine.

"God be with you — forever — and forever — Amen."

And the song increased in volume and splendor and glory—

And I too, was clothed in Light as I kneeled

within the hallway of eternity, as a humble child of earth who became a member of the Church of the Firstborn.

.

VIII.

BEYOND THE LAW OF GRAVITY

The law of gravity, as we have been taught it, applies to the earth and all physical bodies and things: It has been understood in its literal sense as the law of: "What goes up must come down," or fall back again upon the bosom of the earth. This is true as far as it goes, but it does not go far enough.

Every existing thing has its opposite—the night the day— the positive its negative—the north pole its south pole. The very power of creation and existence works according to the two opposite poles or forces. When completed in the full unity of fulfillment, man is not without his mate, for "man is not without the woman, nor the woman without the man, in the Lord." This statement is as far reaching as eternity, for truly nothing exists in creation that is not composed of the two opposite poles or forces of power, masculine and feminine, positive and negative, the light and the dark, or however else one wishes to analyze or express it. In the great divine power of creation and existence these two forces must be. Thus one is not without the other in the Lord, for in these forces are made manifest His powers of creation and of all existing things.

Even the atom is composed of its electrons and protrons, negative and positive charges, operating by the power of God, which is in the midst of all things.

The law of gravity is the negative phase of this plane of existence. It is the female, the night aspect, the electron or negative manifestation of the divine principle. It is the mortal, or physical, or mother aspect of the pole of creation and balance. Gravity is the complete physical action of material existence. It is the law of the earthy, dense, tangible form. It is the law of tangible "matter," which, in most languages, is quite literally "mother." But always, for every existing thing there is its opposite in existence, though not always manifest to mortal understanding eyes.

And always, balanced against the mortal, or physical plane there is the spiritual. Against the law of gravity rests the law of levitation, the spiritual aspect of the eternal law of creation and existence.

The earth, in its massive, physical density, stands heavy and cumbersome. Its rocks and sands compact, immovable, seemingly lifeless in their gross, dead weight. Yet with the touch of the sun and the rain the very soil springs into luxurious growth, imbued with life. The blades of grass, the trees reaching up, ever up. This is the law of the spiritual phase of existence in its minor manifestation. It is the law of growth, of levitation in a milder form, becoming manifest in a very small degree.

And this cumbersome earth itself spins upon its wings in majesty in the midst of the realms of light. It floats upon the wide expanse of space like feathery down in the breeze—yet not blindly is its course wafted by any chance or capricious zephyr. Guided by intelligence, its course is directed and controlled. This floating power, this very speed on wings of light is the opposite pole of gravitation in complete manifestation. This pole is levitation. It is the spiritual pole, as opposed to the physical, mortal, negative pole of gravitation. It is the positive manifestation of the great eternal law of creation and existence.

In its physical manifestation this law of gravity pulls all things belonging to it back to itself. It pulls its children back as they grow old. The very bodies of mankind bend more and more toward mother earth as the years multiply. All physical bodies have been constructed from the elements of earth and will be drawn back into her bosom, in time, if the spiritual end of this great law is not discovered and used by the children of earth, whose feet begin to drag with increasing heaviness as time goes on. The whole physical body begins to sag earthward with greater and greater reluctance to express buoyancy. Even the flesh begins to feel the drawing pull of gravity and deep lines and wrinkles appear. These increase and multiply with time. This sagging flesh of age but manifests the negative pole of existence, the law of gravity in complete action as it fulfills the manifestation of its physical, mortal phase of the great law. It is the law of earth, or the law of gravity that all things shall call unto themselves their own. This is the law of the material phase of existence.

But since all things were created spiritually first there is lying embryo in man also the positive aspect of the great law, the spiritual powers, which are but waiting to be manifest by those who can begin to develop the hidden possibilities waiting to be expressed. As the law of gravity is the negative, or female aspect of the principle of existence, or the manifestation of the mother principle, so it is that as a child matures he slowly grows away from his mother's breast and constant care and more and more develops toward his father's realm of upright independence.

The law of gravity, the law which pulls and draws to itself its own is manifested in mankind just as definitely as it is manifested in earth itself —or in the universe. The law of gravity is the law of matter, tangible substance, physical, mortal existence. And man is a very part of this existence.

This law of the physical is continually manifested in man in the acquisition of earthly things, the accumulation of possessions and wealth as he seeks to draw to himself the things which belong to him by law of effort. In this pulling law of gravity is also the law of repelling the things which are not his own by right. No fortune is gathered illegally without having a curse upon it—or the natural law of its repellent powers. Such wealth can never be held for long. It slips away. It brings no happiness and often it brings disaster.

The light draws to itself the things of light, or, "Light cleaveth to light," and darkness gathers to itself the darkness.

So each individual, according to the strength and power of his being draws to himself his own and unconsciously repels that which is not his by right. If he steals that which does not belong to him he has broken the very lowest law of earthy gravity and the shame for such is very great and the retribution sure. He has outraged the lowest law of mortal being and broken one of the lowest mortal laws, for this reason he is considered lower than mortal. There are many such. Any who are dishonest in the least degree in their dealings with their fellow men are known as sub-mortals. And often these, who are classed among the higher animals are the most lauded among men, though beneath even common, mortal classification.

And all negative tendencies develop more and more the repellent powers against the good. And only the good is happiness, only the good contains the power which is constructive, glorious and filled with everlasting power. Those who accumulate fortunes dishonestly may escape their punishment in this world, but upon their descendants the curse will fall, for all goods gathered illegally carry with them forever the burden of a broken law. Greed is an animal instinct, and when developed, brings the merits of the beasts. To be considered sub-mortal, or sub-human is a status all would escape if they only realized the value of the riches they have forfeited for an empty, temporary, meaningless gain.

To the one who walks in light, with a song of love and gratitude in his soul, the things of light begin to gather. He attracts them to him as definitely as the sun draws back its diffused or scattered energies, as the earth gathers back her dust, the ocean bed its silt, the sea its waters. This is the law of gravity in action. It is a phase of the law of existence manifesting in every mortal, tangible sphere or being. It is the manifestation of the principle which is centered in all things, in the very depths of the soul, in the midst of all things. And the opposite pole is the divine principle of spiritual power—even the power of levitation, to lift, to glorify and to exalt.

Each existing thing has its own center between the poles of gravity and levitation. Man's center is the feeling center in his heart. It is in the very depths of his hidden, inner being. It is balanced according to the thoughts in his soul, or the desires in his heart. If his thoughts are of fear or greed, hate or envy, discord or confusion then that is his own power of gravitation in all its most negative form. And these dark vibrations are his, and the law of gravity will continually recall them to him, multiplied with their tangible, negative burden.

There are some members of society who constantly teeter on the see-saw of these two opposing poles. However, that phase of existence is nearly over. The great outpouring light of heaven will demand that every man find his place, make his choice, either accepting or rejecting the light. There will be no more luke-warm, wavering individuals. They will be either good or bad. And all will be revealed.

If, however, one's heart has developed the great love, where light is centered and developed into a melody or vibration of glory, the crowning gifts begin to be bestowed. Such a one will no longer need to seek for his own, nor strive frantically to hold it to him. Having begun to develop spiritually, or to mature toward fatherhood the greater phase of the higher laws begin to be made manifest. So it is that the great spiritual law of divine love begins to swing one toward the spiritual phase or pole of existence. Perfected love is the complete fulfillment of the great eternal law of being. For such a one the earthly, mortal, physical manifestation or gravitation aspect is fulfilled and he rises above the law. This is the power of the great love or law, as revealed by Paul in his divine revelation on charity. It is the love that suffereth long (without complaint or bitterness or resentment); it is kind; it envieth not; it vaunteth not itself; it is not puffed up (with pride); it doth not behave itself unseemly; *IT SEEKETH NOT ITS OWN;* thinketh no evil; rejoiceth not in iniquity, but rejoiceth in truth."

This is the higher aspect of the law of creation and existence as compared to the negative or gravitational pole. It is a complete *letting go of things,* of *self,* of all negative thoughts and desires. It is a releasing, a giving up. It is the fulfillment of the law that Christ lived, "The Son of Man hath no where to lay His head." And "My kingdom is not of this world," with all the negative aspects, and negative results—and its earthly, clinging, mortal law of gravity. The more possessions one has the greater is the law of gravity upon him.

"For all the law is fulfilled in one word, even in this: Thou shalt love thy neighbor as thyself.

"But if ye be led of the spirit, ye are not under the law.

"The fruits of the Spirit are love, joy, peace, long suffering (or patience), gentleness, goodness, faith, meekness, temperance; *AGAINST SUCH THERE IS NO LAW*." (Gal. 5:13-14, 18, 22 and 23)

Those who can fulfill or develop this great, Christ-like, compassionate, forgiving love have risen above the earthly law and are completely free from it. They are no longer ruled by it. No church on earth can henceforth dictate to them, nor be their guiding law, for the laws of the church have been fulfilled and hence are obsolete, and they are admitted into the higher assembly, even the Church of the Firstborn, the Assembly of Just ones made perfect, even the great Brotherhood of Light.

This is verified by Christ in revealing the great power contained in the two great glorious commandments which truly contain all the laws, and the fulfillment of these two divine laws holds breathtaking, unutterable glory of eternal power, of freedom and majesty—and divinity.

It is the spiritual manifestation of this very law of existence, of "like cleaving like", that fulfills the law of gravity and all things connected with it. Its binding, shackling hold is released, and one becomes free—eternally free. It begins to be manifested first in that inner song of ecstacy, which is but the vibrations of love and praise and gratitude and joy in the heart. It is this vibration of light that lifts one above the mortal, gravitational vibration and begins to spiritualize the very physical body of man. It is an everlasting, singing song of gratitude that makes one glorious, for, "He who is thankful in all things, shall be made glorious; and the things of this earth shall be added unto him, an hundred-fold; yea, more." One becomes freed from the law of earth and needs no longer seek his own. Blessings flow to him, multiplied, glorified and completely spiritualized. In other words, "All things are added unto him," as given in the Sermon on the Mount.

The rich young man who came to Jesus by night had fulfilled all the laws of righteousness but the law of "letting go," the one which releases the last claim of the law of gravity and of earth.

The power to overcome the law of gravity by fulfilling, then rising above it toward its opposite brings forth the spiritual phase of divine power.

The gravitational and levitational opposites of the great law of existence are centered in man's heart. A light heart must be cultivated. And the developing of that singing song of praising, loving gratitude is the perfecting of it. A light heart

is one that has cast its weight and fears aside. The
darkness, the dreariness, the fears must be cast out
by a loving song of devotion. It is when this deep,
singing gratitude and praise is developed so that
it becomes a very part of one's nature that the
higher realm with its glorious vibrations of eternal
light becomes secure. Thus the negative, earthy
pull of gravity has less and less hold. As the light
heart is cultivated and developed one begins to
become glorious. The everlasting song of love and
gratitude, the "Thank You" prayer begins to open
up the regions of light and bestows the power thereof. It is then one truly begins to swing out toward
the spiritual, or positive pole of levitation. As the
heart is guarded this song of joy, or praise and
thankfulness and ecstasy, call it what you like,
begins to develop, the flesh gradually changes and
commences to manifest the spiritual, or levitational
aspect, instead of the negative, gravitational power.
Thus the very flesh, in time, can become completely
spiritualized and the law of levitation becomes
more natural than the physical manifestation of
the lower pole of gravity.

When the heart is heavy the feet are heavy for
the pull of gravity is then in control in its complete physical fulness. When the heart is light the
feet are light and the whole body is buoyant and
joyous. In the very center of one's body is the
balance and the power of complete control.

It was quite necessary to include this information in this record so that the higher laws may be, in a measure, comprehended.

That is why the great glory of the higher, spiritual laws spring into power when man offers to God the heavy burden of his broken heart, which weight, if held, would bind him down forever to the earth with its deadening shackles, its old age, its law of death.

It is when one can *"let go"* and offer his burden to God, with a complete releasing of its binding hold, that one becomes free—free from the negatives, the pull of earth, its continued sorrows, distresses and miseries. As the broken heart is offered freely, willingly, with no strings attached, its burdens are released, glorified and exalted. Man is lifted into the spiritual.

Each burden, each fear, each heartache, each quivering agony of distress and anguish can be thus offered whenever they appear, or accumulate along life's road. And as they are "let go" of, released, without strings or restrictions, to the Lord, they become sanctified and transmuted into unutterable glory and everlasting power. If man could only begin to comprehend the inestimable worth and value of that which he so intensely and violently resents and rejects he would know that within the difficulties' lie the leverage to lift the world. He would kneel in such deep, humble gratitude, thank God with such sincere worship and devotion for every heartache, every tear, every sorrow, for he would realize fully the dynamic magnitude of the power these things contain. Indeed his very gratitude alone would glorify him even if it did not contain the unspeakable power of transmutation, the power to transmute every condition, every sorrow, every heartbreak into shimmering, living light and heavenly power. It is this power which can open the very realms of Light.

It is the law of levitation, or releasing of gravity, connected with the great melody of praising glory singing in their souls that the great assembly, or Brotherhood of Light uses at all times. It is this divine law of levitation that is used by those who work to serve mankind in their fullest capacities as sons of Light, or sons of God, whichever you prefer.

This is the power to come and go as the occasion requires without the need of physical transportation. It is the complete releasing of the earthly, mortal aspect of the law, or of gravity. It is the great freedom for him who knows the truth of the law.

In order to write the remainder of this book so that the mode of service may be, in a small measure comprehended, it is quite necessary to reveal the spiritual aspect of the eternal law of existence.

Fifty years ago scientists proved from a scientific standpoint that it was utterly impossible to develop anything that could transport man through the air. The very law of gravity defied such a possibility. In a small measure those insurmountable barriers of the law of gravity have been conquered on the physical plane.

Only fools deny that which they have not yet experienced. The wise man looks out into the future always with eyes of hope and with an open mind. And his hopes become, in time, the accomplished achievements, the accepted facts of life, tried and tested, tangible and real, for he has proved his hopes and brought them into material manifestation.

Yea, "Prove all things."

IX.

SEALED MINDS

I was back again, living a seemingly normal existence. I even continued in my work for awhile, for only in that way could I reach Martha, and one or two others who were slowly being prepared for light.

At this point one no longer speaks his own words, but receives from that inner source of "all-knowing." Neither does one go forth upon his own, but is called or directed according to the need or the urgency of the demand for help.

There are countless numbers on the earth, at the present time, who seem to be beyond help. Help cannot be forced upon any man. The only way help can be given is for the individual to begin to pull off his seals, and this is difficult unless he will let go of his hates and prejudices and begin to send out love. He must open his heart and mind to the great outpouring light that is gradually increasing in intensity. Its outpouring must be slow and very gradual or it would consume and destroy instead of awakening and developing the latent possibilities in the souls of men. Yet with all this outpouring many are walking in darkness at noonday, and their hearts and minds are remaining completely sealed against light and truth.

And astonishing as it may seem, the most sealed minds are often the "Hallelujah" shouters, the "holier-than-thou" ones, the fanatical religionists, steeped in bigotry and heaped in self-righteousness.

There are those also who are sealed by "the traditions of the fathers." The old-time religions that were good enough for father, grandfather, uncles, aunts and generations of ancestors are not good enough for the coming generation of light. Those old-time religions are as outmoded as the ancient caravan, and as lacking in vitality and efficiency as the covered wagons of the pioneers as compared with modern transportation. The old things have filled their places well, but new things must come. To cling to the old things which were good enough for our ancestors is to hold ourselves back in their era of time, without our making their progress or accomplishing the great things they achieved. We would not only be standing still to pursue such a vain course, we would be going backward. These ideas of holding to the past, its dogmas, its empty rituals, brings forth a dead, lifeless, unprogressive generation living in the utter ruins of past glories, walking only in the hollow, empty footsteps of the great "has been." These are the times that are ours. We must step forth and live in them. Those who cling to the past and the things thereof are the ones that time passes by and life remains a dead experience because it has not been lived.

To such we can give but a passing thought of love and infinite compassion as we go on our way. The great invisible light cannot penetrate that which is sealed. To approach such with spoken words of light and divine reasoning makes them instantly argumentative. Instinctively they feel the need to defend their stand. And instinctively they swing into action on the defensive, using every weapon of words at their command. Their very argumentative attitude is but the complete manifestation of the unprogressive darkness they represent. They raise their voices in order to close their own ears against everything that is not already contained in their sealed minds, lest hearing they would be required to readjust their thinking. This readjustment is most difficult for any who are sealed, either in the traditions of the fathers or in fanatical doctrines. It is easier to live by falsehood than change one's mind, if one does not *love TRUTH* more than he loves life or his own opinions. A sincere, deep *love of truth* permits no seals.

For all who are not open to Light or TRUTH, in its fullest sense, there stands restrictions to progress as definite and as real as solid fortified walls.

which each individual has constructed around himself. Light cannot penetrate such self-made fortifications, for they are constructed of darkness. Only those imprisoned behind such walls can possibly begin to free themselves, by humility, which is that glorious contrite spirit so necessary to progress. This is the offering He requires, along with the offering and sacrifice of the broken heart. A contrite Spirit has to offer, or sacrifice all bigotry, all seals, all prejudices and becomes as open as the heart of a child. Only this contriteness of spirit makes it possible for light to enter, and truth to be revealed.

It takes great courage to give up the ideas one has lived for, worked for, held to and supported and see them crumble into dust and nothingness. Few can face such a seeming catastrophe. This giving up, or letting go of all opinions requires more dynamic courage than most possess. For some it is much easier to relinquish their lives than to give up their opinions. Truth and Light can only enter the heart that is open—the heart that has let go—the spirit that has become humble, contrite and teachable.

The pure religion and undefiled is so simple, so completely beautiful that its very simplicity is a stumbling block to those who pin their pride on show and rituals. Its pure simplicity is perfection, and therefore is not desired, or understood.

True religion does not need the props of great wordy prayers, and learned sermons, it needs no high altars or even magnificent churches, or rich cathedrals. Man is the temple of God and upon his own altar, in the center of his soul, burns the everlasting fire of pure devotion. It is here that the great offering of love is sent forth, where the purity of soul is completely distilled, and the humbleness of heart is developed, and the purity of mind fulfilled. To such the love of one's neighbor is already a perfected reality and it is not an obligation to visit the widows and the fatherless, but a divine privilege. To such, every man is his brother and he loves them even as he loves himself, perhaps more. In his heart the universe is one. Such a one could no more consume great wealth upon his own lusts, while any member of society suffers want, than Christ could have gathered to Himself the thrones of the earth and the riches and honors thereof. The great test the rich young man could not pass is not even a test for such a one.

To serve without hope of reward, or even a desire for it, or a thought of it, is the true service. This is the true law of religion. It is the law of "let not thy left hand know what thy right hand doeth." To give without expecting to be rewarded or hoping to be paid in even the smallest token of appreciation is a part of the great religion.

To serve without honor, or thanks, to serve for the very love of serving, this is the great love. He who works expecting credit, honors, rewards or glory is working for himself, and not for mankind. And his service is inferior and vain. He who demands appreciation for his services is working for even less and inferior pay. To give service and pass on without giving it a second thought, without expecting reward, either in this world, or in the world to come, is the great service, the pure, Christ-like service of complete love. This is the complete releasing of the law of gravity, for in this way one even lets go of the desire for reward—and gives out love from a heart that is full and running over. Service must be rendered entirely through love and because of love—love must be its aim and its end. This is pure religion and undefiled. It is undefiled by empty forms, cumbersome, orthodox rituals, high seats of exalted honors—and many words—This is the religion of everlasting power and light.

In this religion controversial points of doctrine lose their meaning completely. This is the religion beyond race, or color or creed. And into this religion are gathered the noble and great ones of the earth—the kindly Jew, the merciful Mohammedan, the truly understanding Chinese, the unselfish Gentile, the humble, sincere Christian—all those who live the inner laws of righteousness that have been engraved upon the two tablets of man's soul since the world began. This is the law of Israel, which means literally, "Love and Light" —or the sons of Love and Light. These are those who can live the higher laws of Truth—letting go of all else.

This great Truth is beyond creed and dogma and orthodoxy. It isn't a strained, overtaxed, bigoted, contentious, wrangling, monstrous thing fighting against itself. It is the natural cleansing of the inner soul and the progressive march of the great brotherhood of all mankind.

Even the criminal often has a better chance suddenly to swing out into the light than the religious fanatic. The criminal knows in his soul he has failed. And sometimes the very burden of that failure is the balance or power that opens up the heart. Many a criminal, locked in solitary confinement, who in his desperate anguish at having reached the very lowest end of his trail, has suddenly been awakened by the great light and his broken heart has opened to receive. His very soul, has, as in an instant, changed and been exalted and his mind has been enlightened.

From the higher viewpoint it is seen that each person is in the exact place where his most needed lessons can be learned, if he will only learn them. Some are in high positions that they might learn the humility of holding power and many of them fail. Some can only learn by reaching the very lowest point of degradation and shame, some by physical handicaps, deep suffering, poverty or heartbreak. Some in one church, some in another, according to the amount of light and truth the individual is capable of living by, or will accept. Each church has stood in the past to supply some need. The churches were established to help point the way to the higher life, but they have lost the perspective and no longer *point* the way, but claim they *are* the way. Some even assume that they are the entire goal and purpose of existence and the Celestial Authority of heaven itself. At present all are blocking the way with their empty forms, bigoted ideas, powerless priesthoods, orthodoxed creeds of non-expansion, uninspired dogmatism and unbelievable usurpation of the rights of heaven.

It is time to go beyond the earthly churches, beyond the empty phrases, the dead forms, into the Holy-of-Holies in a man's own soul and contact God through individual effort. Each man must begin to do his own praying, his own searching, his own asking—and most of all he must learn to open up his own heart and mind to the great, outpouring of heavenly, divine light that is beginning to enfold the earth with increasing vibrations of everlasting glory. This is the preparation for the baptism of fire and membership in the Great

Church of the Firstborn, which kingdom is not of this world.

Not everyone that saith unto me, Lord, Lord, shall enter into the kingdom of heaven; but he that *doeth the will* of my Father which is in heaven."

X.

THE LISTENING HEART

Here—and there—sitting on a park bench, in a street car, a quiet building, or walking along a busy thoroughfare, or lonely street, a smile can be given, a word passed, or a little nod of appreciation communicated without a word. Invisible rays of living glory, sent out on a kindly thought of infinite love can fortify another with renewed courage and greater power.

Or sometimes it is that a little forgotten soul may pour out his, or her, heart from sheer empty loneliness. Blessed is he who is called to listen to their tales with an understanding heart, for sometimes it is that such unburden themselves to make room for light and love. Often just the call to sit quietly and listen may be the power of bestowing the most divine benediction of all. The gift of listening with an understanding heart is a divine gift which so few have developed.

Little clubs gather over the face of the earth so that each member may again listen to himself tell over again the tales he knows, the things he has experienced or something lived by a friend. Often all talk at once and each is listening only to his own voice, his own words, his own little story which he has heard himself tell many times before. Yet he alone is most interested in it though he knows every word it contains, and the ending of it. And he alone is truly disturbed if he is interrupted in the telling. These things but manifest the lack of truest culture, the art of listening—listening not with the ears only, but with the heart.

This great inner listening does not mean to give ear to idle chatter, to hear only one's own words or waste the energies upon bankrupt minds. This great inner listening eliminates speedily all surface chatter. It develops in each the ability to judge not only the worth of others' conversation, but his own as well. It reveals the value of worthlessness of his own speech, the power or lack of power his words convey and the very depths of his own thoughts.

When the art of listening is cultivated, then it is, that words become sacred, and one's spoken word begins to go forth endowed with divine meaning. They need not be shouted to give them force. Neither need they to be propped up with oaths or flowery phrases to make them emphatic and to clothe them with power and great emphasis. For such a one his "Aye" will mean "aye" and his "nay" will mean "nay." And there will need to be no profane emphasis to substantiate his remarks. None will doubt his words. The world it-self will feel the impact of his speech and give an ear unto his message.

It is the listening heart that is so much needed among men. It is the listening heart that is pre-pared for the full outpouring of the gift of light. It is the listening heart alone that can hear the voice of God.

Listen with your heart and your own speech will become sacred and never again will you trespass upon the patience of your fellowmen by imposing upon them the boredom of your deadly dullness.

This great gift of listening does not mean to give ear to "old-wives tales", empty chatter, de-grading thoughts, belittling words against one's fellow man. It does not mean to waste time upon the vainglorious achievements of someone's past, displayed in wordy pride and self-adulation. It does not mean to give ear to malicious, evil tales, nor to burden oneself with the whining self-pity of some morbid mind. This listening means to learn to hear with the heart, that from the heart of the listener may pour out the light and love of in-finite healing and compassion.

This gift of listening is very sacred, and some-times more useful than the gift of speech.

It is this gift of attentive listening that develops one's "ears to hear." These ears that must learn to hear are the ones deep within the soul. It is first only the power of learning to "feel." This power to feel or listen, develops also deep understanding. While the divine gift of understanding opens the fountains of mercy and compassion, which hold the keys of forgiveness and unspeakable love.

It is this gift of deep listening that one has to develop in order to become a member and be of service in the greater work. The very power to listen holds the keys of divine service, for service is given according to the needs of mankind, the urgency of the occasion and the desires in men's souls. As it is true that the greatest sermons are not always preached in words, so it is true that the greatest needs, the most earnest desires are not always put into uttered prayers. If God never listened what hope would there be for mankind, ever? If the great, noble ones did not listen what possible service could they render, and if man cannot learn to listen how can he possibly be taught by God. Those who do too much preaching, too much teaching, too much talking can never be taught and they will remain in their kindergarten state or grade of existence.

Jeremiah expresses it so beautifully as the following words reveal: "And they shall teach no more every man his neighbor, and every man his brother, saying, Know the Lord, for they shall all know me, from the least of them to the greatest of them, saith the Lord."

Or as John so lovingly expresses it: "But the anointing which ye have received of him, abideth in you, and ye need not that any man teach you; but as the same anointing teacheth you of all things, and is truth, and is no lie, and even as it hath taught you, ye shall abide in it." (I John 2:27).

Or as Christ so perfectly revealed it: "It is written in the prophets, And they shall all be taught of God. Every man therefore that hath heard, and hath learned of the Father, cometh unto me." (John 6:45).

It is this inner ability to be taught of God that is meant by "the ears to hear" given so many times in scripture. The seven seals spoken of in Revelation, chapter five, which only Christ could remove, are the symbolical seals in man's own nature, which only the Light of Christ can release. They are the seals that are placed upon man by his own great wickedness, his sealed ears, that hear not; his sealed eyes, that see not; his sealed mind, that thinks not, seeks not, nor opens to truth; his sealed heart that expands not, but has become barren and hard and unproductive; his sealed soul that has shut out light; and the seals of his own pride and bigotry, woven of self-seeking and greed.

These seals can only be removed as the light of

Christ is permitted to penetrate into the individual and reveal the divine record or rhythm of eternal truth contained within his soul.

Usually the ears that learn to listen open up the way for other of the seals to be removed also. Any one seal removed prepares the way for the removal of others so that eventually all can be cast aside and the great veil of unbelief can be torn asunder.

These seals, as they are removed, reveal glory upon glory, power upon power, realm upon realm, until the very throne of God stands revealed. These seals are upon every man in a more or less binding degree. This great outpouring divine light that is increasing in intensity to reveal all things deep in the hearts of men, will also open the seals within man and bestow all powers if man will only permit it. Man alone makes his choice, judging as worthy or unworthy to receive.

XI

THE MAN IN THE CANYON

One day, not too long after my return from my visit into the higher realms I felt an urgent call of heartbreak coming from across the miles.

In following it I found myself in a deep, Utah canyon, surrounded by high, towering peaks. Majestic crags reached their fingers to the sky. A rushing stream gurgled with spontaneous life as it leaped in exultant laughter over each boulder and stone. Then suddenly it grew hushed and still as an echo of a sob rose from its teary depths. The flowers along its bank bowed their heads in sadness. The tall pines seemed to bow down toward the earth in distressed sorrow as an audible sigh escaped from them. The gigantic mountains stood quivering in pain. The very air grew hushed and still awed by a grief so great.

And then I saw him—a man lying flat upon a mossy bank. His hands dug deep into the soil in convulsive heart rending spasms of anguish. Great heartbreaking sobs shook his being with a sorrow too deep for eyes to witness.

Children can cry and it is but for a moment and will pass.

Women weep and their weeping is an outlet of relief for either joy or sorrow.

But when a strong man weeps with deep, abandoned despair the earth itself groans under the impact of his grief. It shakes the world and rushes on to jolt the universe, and all things stand still and awed and quivering in silence before it. It crumbles the walls beyond the thoughts of men, rends the very atmosphere, and time itself stands still.

This sorrow that is deeper than all meaning is not the weak, shameful, craven sorrow of self-pity. It is not the passing disappointment of a fancy. It is not a temporary, momentary grief. This sorrow is deeper than life itself, beyond existence, as encompassing as eternity. This was the sorrow of the man who threw aside mortality, and standing as a son of God upon the very threshold of eternity laid bare his soul in a grief that demanded a hearing. The man himself was not aware of the great effect nor power of his despair. He could not possibly know how far-reaching and filled with power was that cry of his soul, for that was what it actually was, though he knew it not. Such infinite sorrow receives instant recognition—and I was sent, not that I could really do much about it, except respond in love and enfold him in Light—for I too was to learn a lesson from the experience.

In all my life I had never witnessed such utter anguish, such heartbroken grief, such sobbing suffering. I stood completely awed and trembling before it. I was helpless in the dismay of it, and calling out across the universe told of my need and my inadequacy. I could not even imagine how to begin to give comfort for such grief, let alone justify my intrusion upon it for it was between this man and God.

Then suddenly Annalee Skarin stood beside me. I had met her before. She stood silent for a moment with hand uplifted, and I saw that man's grief registered in her own eyes. It was as though her eyes contained all the suffering of the ages, the heartbreaks of the world, the unspeakable pain of eternities, the sorrows of the entire earth. And I could not bear to look. I turned away and wept as I had never wept before, not even when I heard that Ronnie had been slain. This was a grief deeper than any personal grief. It was the heartaches of all the world gathered into one. That man's grief was Annalee's, it was also mine, but in a lesser degree, though at the time I knew not why. Such grief as this belonged to God for the earth itself could not contain it.

And then there was a great light—and Christ stood there— and kneeling down beside that shaking form He placed His hand upon it—and the weeping slowly stopped—the great, rending sobs

decreased in intensity and finally all was still—
and I heard a blessing given that the earth could
not contain—a blessing of promise, of glory, of
power, of such magnitude that if the physical ears
of the man had heard he would have been consumed. But the ears of his soul heard and a deep
peace came and with it renewed strength and power.

Then Christ sending an unspoken message to us
in love and understanding, smiled and was gone.

Annalee and I withdrew and waited by his car
parked in a dense little grove by the winding,
mountain road. And time picked itself up and
sped upon its way. The stream began to sing again
in deep relief. The trees lifted up their branches
even higher than before in deep murmurs of gratitude. The very mountains relaxed as the tension
vanished, and that whole valley, hallowed by
Divinity, whispered an anthem of loving praise.

The man at last arose, and walking down to the
stream dipped his hands in it to wash off the dirt
that had gathered upon his fingers and packed
under his nails as they had dug into the soil in
his convulsive, unbearable anguish of grief and
agony. He cleansed his hands thoroughly then
washed his face and bathed his swollen eyes. He
lay down upon his stomach and drank from the
running stream. Then rising slowly he lifted his
eyes above the mountains and whispered reverently,
"Thy will, Oh God, not mine be done, only in

some way, please let this be turned to your glory. And be Thou my Judge. Yes, dear God, judge me not according to the judgments of men, but for what is in my heart and for my great love of Thee. I love Thee so!"

Then slowly, very slowly, as if in deep meditation, he came toward his car.

When he finally saw us it was with a feeling of annoyance. He would have retreated but it was too late. He was not only annoyed at our being there but for a moment dismayed at the thought that we might have seen his grief.

Annalee disarmed him in an instant, saying cheerfully, "We hoped the owner of this car would show up before too long." As she spoke there was a smile so warm and a twinkle in her eyes so friendly the man's resentment vanished. The great sorrow she had felt over his suffering had disappeared and I knew that I had been given the sacred privilege of looking deep into the souls of two of God's children—and into the soul of things.

"What's the matter? Did you two get stranded?" asked the man gently.

"It looks that way. Could we ride back to town with you?" I asked.

"Where is your car? Could I help you get it?"

"Oh," I smiled; "that won't be necessary."

"Cars aren't always dependable on these mountain roads. Our transportation is higher up and we can get it later," volunteered Annalee.

"You sure I can't bring it down?"

"Oh no. Don't give it another thought. If we can ride with you we can pick up our transportation later."

We talked casually for the first mile or so, then Annalee remarked; "Have you read the book, 'Ye Are Gods?' It seems to have caused a lot of disturbance here."

He turned and looked at her in a startled way, saying rather cautiously, "Why yes, I've read it. Why?"

"What do you think of it?"

"It can no longer hurt to tell what I think of it," he stated grimly, setting his jaw. "I think it is wonderful! I've read it again and again. There was never another book like it. I'd give my life just for the privilege of believing in anything so beautiful."

"Annalee Skarin told me she was excommunicated from her church for daring to write it," said Annalee gently.

"You knew her then? I would surely like to meet her sometime." The last was spoken with such child-like wistfulness. "She came from Buffalo, New York to visit here in Salt Lake City and it was while she was here she disappeared. That was two years ago. No one has seen her since. Her husband disappeared a short time later."

"You will meet them both before too long, I am sure," promised Annalee. "She would be so proud to know you. She told me that when she was excommunicated that one man was her accuser, her prosecutor, her judge and her jury. That he twisted the things she had written in the book, called it wicked and condemned her for daring to write a book mostly on the grounds that she was an obscure person. If he had written it, or someone else in high places it would have been acceptable, but her obscurity condemned it. He tried to coerce her into recalling it. But how could she when God had commanded her to write it. She knew that the book had been written in flaming glory with a pen dipped in heaven. She always maintained that she could not have written that book in a million years. She was only the humble scribe. Of course she was utterly condemned."

"That is the way we are all treated here who believe in it. The persecution is very great in this area. If it were possible in this day an inquisition would be started and our homes searched for these books—and they would all be burned. It is almost that bad anyway," said the man with infinite sorrow in his voice.

"I understand that in the case of Annalee there was an assembly of men who gathered to witness that shameful proceeding they called justice. That assembly had no voice whatsoever in the trial, nor in the decision. They were men who had never read the book, who knew nothing of its contents, who, without exception had never before in their lives either seen or talked with Annalee before because she had been living in New York for years and had just arrived in the city. And most of those men were so flattered at being called into such an assembly and so overwhelmingly awed by that presiding authority they could not even think."

"Yes, it must have been terrible for her."

"She told me that her heart broke. She was filled with such inconsolable sorrow she felt she could never be comforted. Her very life seemed to crumble into ashes and dust around her. It seems she had given her life to her church, her time, her talents, her strength, a tenth of her income, and for a time, even half of all she earned. She had taught classes for years, headed organizations, filled missions and had never received a dime, or for that matter, even a 'thank you' for her service. It had been her very life. And of course it was through such a complete, self-sacrificing service that the very heavens were opened and light began to be poured out upon her. Her book was written in fire and tears. She said she wept almost from beginning to end with the glory of it and it was as though she were enfolded in flames of fire as light poured down through her and out upon the pages in the typewriter. That marvelous book was written in one month and no one ever felt more awed or humble about it than Annalee. It was because she stepped beyond those in charge, who only seemed to be blocking the way, that she was cast out. The shame of her trial is written on the archives of eternity along with all such shameful trials which have blackened the records of time.

"She said her grief was impossible to bear until she weighed it carefully against the truth God had revealed. She had felt that it would have been a relief to have been stoned to death for the privilege of believing in a God of such dynamic power, and in the promises He had made. She was sure that burning at the stake could have been a divine privilege—but being cast out of her church was the great, seemingly impossible sacrifice. Her life would have been so easy to have given in comparison.

"It was when her grief had spent itself, so I've been told, that a new understanding and power came. And lifting up her heart she prayed, 'Dear God, forgive my sorrow. And now, with all my heart, I thank you, gracious Father, that I had something more precious to me than my life to offer to you for the price of these eternal truths. Thank you, dear God, that I had something as precious and sacred to me as my membership in this church to give.'"

"Good heavens!" gasped the man when she had finished; "Only the one who wrote a book so great could understand the privilege of such complete suffering and turn it into glory.

"You see, I just went up into that canyon to pour out my heart for having lost my standing in my church because I believe in that book. I just knew I couldn't go on living. My family, my friends have all turned against me. It is almost as though I had leprosy. And, now, thanks to you, I am grateful! How wonderful it is, really. Yes—it is wonderful to have something more precious than your life to give."

"Yes, isn't it?" I marveled softly, regretting almost that I had not been required to make such a supreme sacrifice because I had belonged to no church.

In that afternoon it was revealed to me the great price that is required to bring truth to the earth. I rejoiced that there are those who are willing to pay such a price for it. I knew that as long as these noble and great ones tread the earth God's power will rule, and eventually triumph over all the bigotry, injustice, pride and narrowed prejudices of men.

Then Annalee said, "I have heard that Annalee was finally told that it was not her trial they held at all, but their own. They had tried themselves as surely as those who had condemned Joan of

Arc. And the record of their injustice would stain the earth, as thousands have done since time began, until the earth itself is cleansed. The shame of such mockeries will be completely revealed before the end—and before the complete cleansing comes."

We were now entering the city, one of the most beautiful cities in the world, tucked in at the foot of the mountains.

We had gone but a few blocks into the city when Annalee said, "Please stop here. This is where we will be leaving you—and thank you so much for the ride."

"It is I who should thank you. It has been a privilege to have had you with me. It seems almost as though you were directed to me."

"Yes, doesn't it?" I smiled.

"I hope I see you again. Here take my card. It has my telephone number and address. Let me know if you get your car all right.

After he had shaken hands with us he seemed loath to go.

"What are your names?" he asked.

"Mine is Christine Mercie," I volunteered.

"And I am just here for the day, but I shall see you when I come to Salt Lake City again," promised Annalee.

At last the car moved on leaving us standing there.

XII

ANNALEE AND REASON SKARIN

Often the helpers who are sent to assist are not visible to mortal eyes. The man in the canyon did not see or hear the loving tender benediction and blessing of Christ. He only felt it and his grief was healed because his heart was opened to receive. And though many of the great and noble ones may remain invisible nevertheless the help is just as real. The members of the great Assembly of Light have so perfected themselves through unselfish love that their vibrations are so high they are not visible to those on the mortal plane—unless the mortals are quickened by the Spirit of God, and thus their consciousness can be raised so that they can behold with their eyes.

Annalee was sent to help me with the brother grieving in the canyon because she had experienced the very thing he was experiencing and for the same reason. It was her work. I was only privileged to witness and be a very humble observer to a drama so great that I might be given greater understanding.

"Annalee," I asked after we were alone, "Why couldn't you give your name just now?"

"Our brother would have forgotten the blessing he received over his excitement in having seen me. They insist upon giving me credit for this work. I have tried to tell them that no credit is due me. Only God could reveal a work so great. I feel so completely humble—and even now I am overwhelmed with awe by a record so divine."

"But why can't you return yet to these who must be so anxious to see you again?"

"I would have remained with them in the beginning, except they would have relied on me too much. In this work, as you know, each person must learn to stand upon his own feet, and in his own strength. This is the day in which no man can give of his oil to another. No one can carry another through. It is a work as completely individual as being born and dying. It is like the kernel of wheat planted in a field. Alone it must unfold and find its strength in the dark bosom of mother earth. Alone it must find the power to begin to expand. Alone it must reach up to the light with infinite seeking and heart-breaking (shell breaking) desire to overcome the darkness. Then when it has matured enough to stand alone in the glorious realms of light it finds itself a part of the whole.

"Any individual who has to depend on another

for his, or her knowledge, strength, testimony and inspiration can never enter into the great realms of Celestial light—not worlds without end. That is the meaning of: "Cursed is he who trusteth in the arm of flesh, or maketh flesh his arm." This is a curse indeed. It is a curse so devastating that it has held the world in darkness for generations upon generations. It has cancelled the command to all men, "ask, seek and knock." It has stifled thinking. It has sealed progress. It is damnation— and truly cursed is he who fails to develop his own light, fails to find God through his own efforts, for in no other way can He possibly be known. And it is indeed a curse to any man who fails in his own great quest. He must do his own seeking, his own searching, and asking, and most of all HIS OWN THINKING.

'It is for this very reason that I could not remain among those I love so much. And now there are some of them, who by their own awakened faith and their own efforts, are almost prepared to receive the great anointing and be ushered into the eternal light."

"Can't you return to some of them individually?" I asked hopefully

"Not yet, Christine. If we did that it would have more meaning for them than the great message we left them. And that would likewise be disastrous. We dare not think of our great love for them too strongly lest we stand before them before it is time."

"We?" I asked.

"Yes. Reason, my beloved one, and I. He was as much a part of this work as I. He gave all that he had to give for it, and almost more. We are usually together. Just occasionally there are assignments we fulfill alone. He is so very wonderful."

"I have never even heard of him, I should like to meet him."

"And you shall." She had no sooner spoken than a man stood beside her. "This is Reason," she said turning to me.

"Yes. He is wonderful".

Later I learned that their love was a proverb in the great Celestial realms—How it had endured across time and space from the very beginning of existence—and in mortality it spanned the years and a continent—and a lifetime, for they waited for twenty-three years, after meeting on earth, for the privilege of being together.

XIII.

THE POWER OF GREAT LOVE

There are those in mortality who think love is a weakness. Love is not a weakness. Love is strength.

It is definitely true that to those who love much, much can be forgiven.

This love can be cultivated until it rises above every trial and every temptation. It is power released that can endure all things, rejoice in all things and glorify all things.

To him who has perfected love there is no such thing as fear. He has overcome the very power of fear. To such a one there is only a love of God so great and all-inclusive that it is all there is left. And this love builds a wall of light around the individual that is pure, penetrating glory. For such a one there are no evils, for they no longer can touch him. If evils should come to one who has perfected love the evils are instantly transmuted into blessings and glory and light, such is the power of love. One who has perfected the great gift of love deserves God's will to be done more than he wants anything else

in existence, every personal desire vanishes before
a love so great. Even a desire to be freed from
suffering, no matter how great that suffering is,
is completely banished. He wants only God's
will to be done to the extent he has no other desires in his soul. This is the pure, divine, Christ-
like love that is completely exalted.

When one has this perfected love he can endure
any suffering, any heartbreak or seeming calamity.
In the most excruciating pain or torture he can
lift himself above it through his love. The pain
can be the same, throbbing with the same intensity, but through his love he can detach himself
from it. He will be aware of it still; can even
analyze it and accept it, for it can still remain a
part of the physical body. He can know it is there.
He does not deny it any more than Christ needed
to deny the crown of thorns, nor the reality of the
cross. But by the great gift of love he can rise
up above the physical, and from the spiritual
observe the suffering, and praising God for it,
can heal it forever. This is the power of healing
—and the great healing will follow as the day
follows the night. It is transmuted into added
strength and power.

It was the great power of this divine love that
Christ used when He stood in such majesty while
a crown of thorns was crushed upon his brow,
while he was mocked and jeered, spit upon and

crucified, then said, "Father, forgive them, for they know not what they do." This is the love that every individual has the right to. This love perfected is the majesty and power of God.

Few understand that it is man who receives the great blessing when those two first and great commandments are fulfilled literally. It is man's ills that are healed. It is to him the great strength comes, and to him the power is given. It is to the one who learns of the great love, and perfects it right within his own soul that the complete healing comes—the great renewal.

When he fulfills the second great commandment, to love his neighbor as himself, then comes the power to heal one's neighbor.

These two commandments cannot be fulfilled in a minute, nor a day. It takes time to plant the desire for this great love. And even before the desire there must be a partial vision and an understanding of it. After the desire is planted it takes more time to cultivate it until it is perfected. That great love must be practiced constantly until the heart, the soul and the mind have learned to co-operate in vibrating with it and then in sending out. And it is when this love has become the very meaning and purpose of existence that life begins to have the divine powers made manifest and can shake off mortality and ascend into the realms of light.

It is when one has so perfected this love that there can be no more discord, no more confusion, no more weakness or fears that one realizes how completely his heart has become softened. And it is then the veil of unbelief is rent.

It is then that one not only perfects this great love. He actually becomes it. He *is* love.

There is no possible way to express the magnificent power and glory of such a condition. One can only begin to comprehend it when he has planted the desire to fulfill it in his own heart.

The clearer one's vision becomes in viewing this love and the wonder and power of it, the keener becomes his desire to fulfill it. When the acquisition of this great, unspeakable gift becomes the one and only aim, when it has become a burning obsession that can no longer be denied, then it will be fulfilled.

To the one who perfects this divine gift of love the realms of Light open wide and all powers will be bestowed—beauty in all its Celestial perfection, health in all its full magnificence, divine strength in its purified rhythm of majesty, and power in its illimitable fullness.

This is the love of God. This is the love beyond all gifts. This love is perfection in its fullest extent and scope. "Pray to God with all the energy of heart that ye might be possessed of this great, divine, Christ-like love." Let this love begin to sing as a melody of thanks in your heart. Worship and praise and adore and let your hearts be lifted up continually in songs of everlasting joy and the love will be yours—yea, all things and all powers will be yours, whether in heaven or on earth.

XIV.

THE GREAT GLORY

There are many great and divine ones who tread this earth unknown and unrecognized by the mortals they contact. These great and noble ones, from the realms of light, remain in contact with the earth that they might help all who are prepared to receive help. Their mission is of selfless service to a world so that darkness might be dispelled and the great, full Light of God shine into the hearts of men.

There is no individual on this earth who has not been contacted by one or more of these holy ones, who have come to them, appearing as ordinary mortals, hoping to find some response in that contact by which greater light might be given.

More and more these divine ones are seeking to serve, for there is not too much time remaining in which the earth must get into line with the great purposes of God. And "by the earth" is meant all humanity.

Many of the more spiritually advanced are able to recognize these great helpers. And by their own

enlightened progress they are able to receive constant help from the higher realms of Light.

No one who sincerely calls is left without an
answer. But many are completely unprepared to
recognize the answer. Because of blindness of
mind, bigotry, selfishness or pride it is often impossible to recognize the great help that is always
at hand. One has to be attuned to the higher vibrations of unselfish love in order to comprehend
the great and unspeakable power continually offered for every need. This power is available to
all, from the greatest to the least. One has but
to accept it.

The scriptures tell us that Christ died for our
sins. He truly died *because* of our sins. And the
Light of Christ within each of us is crucified afresh
by our sins even to this day. As long as that
Light is not permitted to come forth and become
active in our lives, to that extent HE lies dead
within us because of our sins. And to that extent
we are unable to enter into the great Church of
the Firstborn and become living members in the
divine Brotherhood of Light. This membership is
reserved for those who have been tested and tried
in all things and have proved that they will serve
HIM at all hazards instead of their own selfish
aims, proud lusts and empty vanities in order to
surpass in glory and exaltation all others along
the road.

The first requisite in this holy Assembly is the complete putting aside of the self with its jealousies and unholy pride and lusts.

It is unimportant whether we, individually, receive a great reward or not. He who works for reward is working for a menial's pay. He who serves to surpass all others is placing leaden weights upon his own feet and barring his own way. He is traveling the way of self and it is a "dead end" road—a road that ends in self.

He who serves only for love, without thought of reward, becomes the greatest, for he has placed himself as the least and the servant of all, not through a desire for reward or for glory or for honor, but unselfishly to help lift mankind to greater heights. Such a one would gladly sacrifice himself, and all thought of reward just for the humble privilege of helping his fellow men ascend into the light. Such a one is a literal son of God.

Know this, oh, man, there are those who have not earned any place whatsoever in the great realms of eternity. There are those who are but servants and these are those who are working entirely for rewards and hopes of glory. They are but menials and their reward is a servant's pay. Then there are those who are members of the Father's household. These work not for reward, but for love. They think not of glory nor of self but only in loving devotion sacrifice themselves for the uplift of all. Of this divine group is composed the great Assembly of Light—the divine ones, sons of God, whether in mortality or out of it. He who glorifies in any position or office is receiving his reward in his own satisfaction and gratified pride. He is a menial, a common servant, not a son, not a member of the divine household.

The bickerings of churches over which is nearest to God—or which is God's most Holy Church is as empty and vain as the argument of the apostles of old over who would sit on His right and who on His left. Churches have very little meaning except to keep alive a knowledge of God on the earth. It is true that some churches have more truth than others. But no church has ALL TRUTH. If there was such a church it would have ALL POWER and every member would be able to do the works Christ promised to those who believe.

Some churches are only fanatical works of darkness.

Every church that is not leading its members into those greater powers, promised by the Son of God, is but blocking the road of progress. Such churches permit none to attain to a point beyond the organized mass of their orthodoxed conformity. Such churches have so completely sealed the doors of progress to their members that they are but instruments of damnation. Some have placed deadly seals upon the minds of men, permitting none to approach God except through themselves, who are but blocking the way of light. They deny the power of God and the gift of the Holy Ghost even while claiming that they alone possess the authority to bestow such a divine gift. Such claim loudly that they alone on the earth possess the authority to bestow the Holy Ghost, by the laying on of hands, and at the same time deny that those on whom they bestow such divine power have any ability to use the gift and the powers it contains. They deny that this great and Holy Gift of the Spirit can lead anyone into ALL truth, for only they, themselves can do that. If any humble individuals reach out to God for answers, and receive them, such answers are disclaimed and pronounced evil. Thus they deny the power of God to answer the prayers of the humble and contrite and deny the *power* of the Holy Ghost to fulfill its purpose. Those who place such seals on the way of progress permitting none to reach out beyond the stymied, orthodoxed leaders who live only on the traditions of the fathers and not according to the power of God will shortly be called into judgment.

As the great house of God is put in order the cluttered useless teachings shall be replaced by the great living principles of active power and light. And no man will need to be taught henceforth by his neighbor, brother, priest, bishop or minister, but all will be taught of god.* It will be the great living power of God active in every individual. His Spirit shall be poured out upon all flesh and there will be none left who can claim any monopoly upon it or retard this great power. Those who cannot humble themselves before such divine and Almighty power will be removed from their places, for a knowledge of the Lord shall cover the earth even as the waters cover the sea. And those who have tried to substitute their own wisdom and personalities to take the place of this power in the lives of men will be humbled or destroyed.

Nevertheless, judgment is an individual thing. It is based upon each individual's will to serve and how well he has lived up to the principles of righteousness that issue out of his own heart. His place is selected according to his capacity to give out love, not on any office held on earth or any coveted position occupied in pride and splendor. Service only is accepted which is offered in purest love and deepest humility, without thought of reward. It is this great, selfless service of divine love one must give if he wishes to attain to the membership in the great Assembly of the Firstborn.

"Your sins have separated you from me," pro-

---

* (I John 2:27; John 6:45 and Jer. 31:31-34)

claimed the great Isaiah in giving forth the words of the living God. Our sins are still separating us from Him. He has not walled or shut us out. We have shut ourselves out. Through our lusts and pride and jealousies and secret covetings and selfishness we have separated ourselves from Him and his divine power of perfect fulfillment.

Membership in the great Assembly or Church of the Firstborn is based entirely upon complete unselfishness and perfect love. These are the requisites necessary to be numbered among the great and holy ones who offered themselves as a ransom to help lift the world. This is the love Christ spoke of—the love which a man is willing to give, even his life, that his brother might be spared. It is the love that is willing to forego all rewards to exalt another. It is the great love that makes a man willing, if required, to sacrifice even his own soul to glorify the whole. This is the pure, divine, Christlike love. This is the love Christ meant. This love is of the soul and is gloriously divine. This is the love that has all the power of fulfillment. This is the love which, when developed, makes one a true member of the great Assembly, a literal son of God, for he is then born of God, not in mere symbolism, but in actuality. Baptism in water is but the shadow of the symbol.

That great and noble son of God who attained

with glory a membership in the Great Church, the writer of the Odes of Solomon, which are so beautifully recorded in the New Testament Apocrypha, explained it so perfectly in his 26th Ode, as follows:

"Who is able to interpret the wonders of the Lord?

"For he who could interpret would be dissolved and would become that which is interpreted."

If one perfects love he will become that love. If he perfects humbleness and gratitude he will become the Great Attitude of love and power.

Each year Annalee and Reason Skarin, at Christmas time, offered a Birthday gift to the Son of God. One year it was Love, another, the singing song of ecstasy from deep within their souls—a song of joyous devotion that dispelled and destroyed darkness. One year it was the gift of gratitude and thanks which released continual praise from within their hearts.

After each gift was offered they sought with all their power to perfect it—Love, Joy and Gratitude and thus each gift became a living gift—a gift of everlasting value. And the gifts held the power to fulfill the offering.

It is everyone's privilege to fulfill and become the gift he offers or the whole thing he interprets. "Interpret the wonders of the Lord and be dissolved and become that which you interpret." Such is

the power within each and every individual on this
earth to glorify his soul and to become a member
in the Great Brotherhood of Light.

XV

THE GREAT ATTITUDE

"Blessed are the poor in spirit; for theirs is the kingdom of heaven." Yea, blessed are those who become the attitude of loving humility for to them will be opened the great kingdom of expansion. An attitude that is held becomes a reality. And "Beatitude" means literally to *be the attitude*. Being that attitude fulfills it and the reward it contains.

Be in the attitude of mourning, not in self-pity or angry rebellion, but through sincere sorrow, and you will be comforted—or receive that divine and Holy Comforter Whom the Father sends to all who mourn. The gift is always sent to those who mourn but there are few who accept of His comfort, for they love darkness and their sorrows and misery more than they love Light. But no one ever mourns who is not offered this great divine comfort.

"Blessed are the meek," or those who become the attitude of meekness, "for they shall inherit the earth." And this does not mean to carry a false attitude of meekness and humility. It means actually to BE that attitude. Neither does it mean that they shall inherit the earth in some great, far-off "hereafter." It means here and now—for all things will become subject unto them, for they will have learned obedience. And by their obedience they become willing to let God's will be done. And only God's will is perfection. And it is His will to bestow all gifts and blessings on those who have learned true obedience or meekness.

"Blessed are they which do hunger and thirst after righteousness: for they shall be filled (with the Holy Ghost)" says one translation. And it is definitely sure that when one truly hungers and thirsts after righteousness he is going to ask, seek and knock until his desire or craving is appeased. And the bestowal of the Holy Ghost is the gift that leads to all knowledge and into all truth. Therefore, to become the very attitude of seeking and searching and desiring fulfills the promise that everyone who asks receives; and he who seeks finds; and unto him who knocks it shall be opened. It also proves that such a one is not already so burdened with seals and convictions that he already possesses all truth and all righteousness. It is the great open invitation of the soul seeking to be taught. Those who are already convinced that they possess all righteousness, and all knowledge concerning it, have damned their own progress. The very attitude of hungering for perfection helps to fulfill it.

"Blessed are the pure in heart: for they shall see God." When the heart is completely pure then can the great love of God be so perfected in it that God will be revealed. This is a promise that automatically has to be fulfilled as the conditions are met.

Thus as one *becomes* the attitude necessary to live up to and fulfill the requirements the great promises unfold in all their divine glory here in this life.

And now, leaving the listed Beatitudes for a moment let us discuss the greatest of all attitudes. This one *is* gratitude. Gratitude is the Great-Attitude. It is that glorious song of thankfulness, or praise and joy and love that opens the very windows of heaven and fulfills the great promises mentioned so often by Annalee Skarin, that: "He who is thankful in all things shall be made glorious; And the things of this earth shall be added unto him, even a hundred-fold, yea more."

Become this Great Attitude of singing devotion and praise and all things shall be added unto you, both in heaven and on earth. This is the deep joy and gratitude that desires only God's will to be done, that rejoices in anything that He brings —and in that joy and rejoicing and obedience all things are transmuted into blessings and glory and power and complete perfection. And it is this attitude that overcomes darkness and the powers thereof.

Such is the meaning of His words and such is our power of fulfilling them.

Yea, "Blessed are you when men shall revile you, and persecute you, and shall say all manner of evil against you falsely, for my sake," if you will but rejoice and be exceeding glad. The blessing comes not in the persecution but in the attitude of gratitude and gladness and in the rejoicing. This great love and thanksgiving in God's will being done contains the very keys of heaven. It holds the keys of knowledge and understanding that one is having the privilege of being tested and tried (in all things) that he might be permitted to enter with great honors into the great Assembly of Light. Such persecution should bring the greatest joy to the human soul and will if rightly understood. But know that it is not the persecution nor the reviling that contains the promise, or the blessing—it is the attitude in which they are received.

This Assembly or the Church of the Firstborn is composed of "Those who overcome by faith, and are sealed by the Holy Spirit of promise, which the Father sheds forth upon all those who are just and true.

"They are they who are the Church of the Firstborn.

"They are they into whose hands the Father has given all things—

"They are they who are priests and kings, who have received of his fullness, and of his glory . . .

"These are they who have come to an innumerable company of angels, to the general assembly and Church of Enoch, and of the Firstborn . . .

"They who dwell in his presence are the Church of the Firstborn; and they see as they are seen, and know as they are known, having received of his fullness and of his grace:

"*And He makes them equal in power, and in might, and in dominion.*"

And these who are admitted into the Church of the Firstborn "Are ordained unto the holy order of God, to administer the everlasting gospel; for they are they who are ordained out of *EVERY* nation, kindred, tongue and people BY *THE ANGELS* TO WHOM IS GIVEN POWER OVER THE NATIONS OF THE EARTH, to bring as many as will come to the Church of the Firstborn."

And those who fulfill all laws and "Keep all commandments will have the heavens opened unto them, and be able to commune with the general assembly and Church of the Firstborn, and to enjoy the communion and presence of God the

Father, and Jesus the mediator of the new covenant."

Yea, "If thou shalt ask, thou shalt receive revelation upon revelation, knowledge upon knowledge, tnat thou mayest know the mysteries and peaceable things—that which bringeth joy, and that which bringeth life eternal."

Then know that prayers are answered, desires fulfilled when it is possible to ask without doubting in one's heart. They are fulfilled when one literally becomes the attitude that fulfills the law. When the doubts are conquered by love then faith is perfected and the attitude is established. When you can get the feeling that you actually possess the gifts you require, without doubting, they will be yours completely and fully. It is the feeling, or the attitude, not the thinking which brings the fulfillment. It is the power of holding to an attitude until one becomes that attitude which fulfills it. *Be* the attitude of meekness, not occasionally, but *be* it and its promise shall be yours. *Be* grateful and you shall become that greatest of all attitudes, the great powerful fulfillment of gratitude and will be made glorious and the things of this earth shall be added unto you, even a hundred-fold; yea more. Rejoice and be exceeding glad when persecution comes, which is one of the greatest human tragedies when considered on the surface, but one which holds the examination papers for graduation with honors—the certificate of membership among the prophets of old. For thus were the prophets persecuted before you—and so was their reward.

It is these great ones who sacrificed themselves gladly and with great joy for the enlightenment of the whole who make up the great membership of the Assembly of Light. These are the ones who were willing to lay down their lives for their friends, even to the complete sacrificing of themselves, their positions, their honor, their reward and hope of glory even that Truth might shine forth in ever greater brilliance to light the way of the wandering footsteps of their fellow men.

Back in 1512 Erasmus said: "The yoke of Christ would be sweet if petty human institutions had not added to the burden . . . Yea, would that people let Christ rule through the command of His word, and not try to build their tyranny with human decrees."

Seek not to know God through churches or men or leaders, but seek God through your own heart and through your own divine attitudes fulfill His holy promises. Perfect these holy attitudes and you will be dissolved and will become that which you interpret. Seek to become love in all its compassionate, divine, forgiving, Christ-like mercy and you will know the mysteries of Godliness—or the great mystery and power of becoming Godly.

XVI.

"FORGIVE US OUR DEBTS AS WE FORGIVE OUR DEBTORS"

The great powers hidden behind the words contained in the Sermon on the Mount have been lost upon our human ears.

Suppose we take the words contained in the Lord's Prayer, "Forgive us our debts as we forgive our debtors," and apply them literally in our lives. In order to understand their full meaning it is necessary to go behind the words. We must search for the inner meaning of a law so divine its very blinding glory has sealed our eyes with its brilliance and kept us from beholding clearly its infinite power of redemption.

We quote the prayer with our lips but our minds have comprehended it not. Our eyes have seen not and its power and meaning has not penetrated into our hardened hearts and the prayer has remained empty and meaningless in our lives.

If we carry with us through life and on into the next world, which we will do unless we rid ourselves of them here, our hates, our envyings, our discords, our confusion and jealousies and greeds, we will be as completely bound with them as we are at the present time. And the chains with which they bind us are the very chains of hell.

Contained in this most powerful of all prayers is the law that can deliver us from these chains of darkness and set our feet upon the pathway of eternal light and our feet will be forever glorified for the law is ours and the power thereof.

It is a simple law yet its power is beyond anything man has ever experienced. In this day and age, in particular, it is considered smart to retaliate to every harsh word, every unkind act. It is considered a dumb and stupid thing to let slights pass by unavenged. And this road of vengeance is gathering up the whole human race as it struggles along blindly under its burdens of discords, darkness and intensified confusion.

If one would forgive as he hopes to be forgiven—or better still, forgive solely for the sake of forgiving, he will soon be lifted beyond the powers of darkness. He will have the power to enter the kingdom of heaven and to abide in its blessings.

He who will learn to replace the desire of retaliation with a silent blessing will know the true meaning of the word power, for it will be given to him. He will cease to carry around with him his burdens of dislikes, hates and smoldering, unkind thought. Instead, he will carry only love and compassion and mercy and the power of understanding. And ere he is aware of it he will find himself clothed in light, which light is the white raiment spoken of in scripture and the shame of his own nakedness or sins will never appear. Slowly, gradually, like dropping off one by one the defiled rags of darkness he will find himself cleansed and purified and arrayed in eternal light and power.

Each dark thought one leaves behind lifts his own burden of sins and transgressions. If he can get the vision of the great blessing that is his he would never for an instant hold a grudge or any unkind thought against any living thing, especially a fellow being. His own power of redemption is in his own hands for as surely as he forgives he will have the power to be forgiven for the law is his own. It is his to use or to reject. With each hate unreleased, each unkind thought clutched to his breast he is wearing the dark garments of his own transgressions for they are interwoven with his own grudges and dislikes. The burden of his every mistake, weakness and sin is a very part of his own confusions and envyings and bitter hates. This fabric is all one and the same thing and man is clothed completely in its repulsive darkness. As he casts himself the burden of his neighbor's errors, his enemy's mistakes, his acquaintances' trespasses he will surely shed his own weaknesses, his own transgressions and his own sins. Just by forgiving he can shed the darkness and stand freed from every mortal obligation and blundering mistake, every intentional, dishonest act, every hidden weakness. He will be clothed in the power of light. Majesty will be his—the very majesty to say, even in the most tragic abuse, "Father, forgive them. They know not what they do." These are not just words. They are divine power in action—the power that is every man's right to use.

"Lord, forgive us our debts as we forgive our debtors" is a law and contains a promise that cannot be broken. It is power such as few have ever dreamed of. It is a gateway into the higher realms of existence for in it is also contained the power of the First and Second Commandments. As one forgives he learns the power of love—and that power will open up to him the very realms of heaven—for in these two commandments are contained all the laws and the prophets. All the laws and all the prophets means the fulfilling of every divine law ever given and the receiving of every blessing promised by every prophet to mankind since time began. Every dynamic promise of the scripture can be fulfilled by these laws. Every promise of every prophet is his who will fulfill the law. If there is any promise in scripture, or in existence, for that matter, that you desire, then lay hold of these laws, live them and you shall receive in complete fulfillment any blessings your heart can possibly desire or yearn for.

As one forgives he loses his powers of hate and learns the ineffable power of love, the divine majesty of it and the unspeakable glory of it.

"Love your enemies. Pray for those who despitefully use you and persecute you." Forgive all, instantly and completely and you will walk with God and become associated with those great and noble ones whom God has reserved unto himself.

These laws of forgiveness and love contain greater power than the atomic bomb. Its power ends in a flash of destruction. The power of love and forgiveness belongs to any who choose to use it and it endures forever. Not one tiny shred of it can ever be lost or destroyed. These laws of God belong to all, to rich and poor, strong and weak, ruler or slave. And to each who fulfills them the ineffable power of eternal freedom and majesty is waiting and robes of glorified light will be his. The shame of his own nakedness, the very shame of his own sin and weaknesses will be completely dissolved in the power of forgiveness.

Yes, God forgives whom He will forgive. He forgives those whom his law of forgiveness forgives. If any fulfill that law they are automatically forgiven. This is his law of forgiveness. This alone is God's law of forgiving and he has be

stowed it upon man. It is the law of the universe
and applies individually to every human being.
God forgives those whom his law forgives, or those
who have fulfilled the law—and of us it is required to forgive all men. That is how his great,
merciful law of forgiveness works. It is as simple
as that. As real and literal as that and as eternal
and powerful as that. He forgives whom He will
forgive, or whom his law forgives. Fulfill the law
and be forgiven. He has invited all to come to
him who labor or who are heavy laden with mortal
sins and mistakes and burdens and He will give
complete rest. But it is only possible to come
to him through the fulfilling of his laws. His *laws
are* his WILL and they contain the unspeakable
power of every promise ever given.

God never gave one law for his own personal
glory or satisfaction. But every law is given that
they might glorify man and clothe him in light
and majesty. The laws are given that man might
use his own free agency in becoming perfect, even
as God is perfect. These laws are that man might
receive power even as God has power.

Forgive and you shall be forgiven and stand
purified before the very throne of God, clothed
in light and majesty and eternal love, walking with
God—a member of the great assembly of Light.
This law is one of the most exact, the most posi-

tive and definite laws ever given to man—and God is no respecter of persons. He who fulfills this law shall receive the promises—forgiveness—power —light—and the keys of eternity.

XVII.

SO LET IT BE

So ends this record I have been permitted to write.

There may be a series of records to follow this one, for there is enough material to write many volumes such as this—enough material to fill the earth books—but not all of it can yet be written.

To you who receive this work, I would ask that you seek to fulfill the things it explains, for they are true. Learn to be grateful in all things, even heartbreak, and transmute it into glory and power through praise and thanks. Worship and adore, not in fanatical words and actions, but with a song of inner gladness and eternal praise.

Offer your burdens to the Lord with a complete releasing trust, and know that they can be thus changed into blessings.

Rend the veil of unbelief. Let your hearts be softened with tenderness and divine, compassionate, Christ-like love. Perfect the gift within your souls, along with a contriteness of spirit. Train your hearts to melt and your mental "eyes to see" beyond the physical manifested world of solid and concrete things. Then the veil can be rent for the unbelief will be completely overcome.

Learn the power of the law of gravity, its place in the physical world, and develop the power to subdue and overcome it. Learn the power and reality of the spiritual law of levitation and it will be yours to use.

Open wide your hearts and souls and minds to the great Light being poured out without measure. Gather it in and multiplying it in your souls, send it out to help heal a world.

And until we meet in person, God be with you—
CHRISTINE MERCIE.